Politics in The Gambia and Guinea-Bissau

This book explores how pre-colonial political traditions and practices shape modern-day politics in The Gambia and Guinea Bissau. The precolonial Kaabu empire dominated the region for over 300 years, leaving a rich oral and ritual culture that emphasized the importance of a ruler's legitimacy among the general population. This book traces how postcolonial political administrations and Justice, Integrity and Truth (JIT) movements have mobilized to reclaim, reinvent and subvert traditional Kabunka norms of statecraft to prove their political legitimacy. It shows how cultural memory, oral arts and musical forms can be used to express ideals of leadership and followership and, in the process, create various conversations and debates about politics and society, social attitudes and morality. In doing so, the book captures how the latent but influential social and political practices from Kaabu are reclaimed, reproduced or subverted to contribute to the evolving nature of political rhetoric in these two countries.

Whereas many studies of the state in Africa take Western democratic principles as a starting point, this book provides important evidence on the continuity of precolonial political culture along African's west coast. It will be of interest to researchers studying politics, history and anthropology both within the region and elsewhere in Africa.

Mariama Khan is a Gambian scholar, poet and cultural advocate. She teaches at Lehman College, New York. She is the author of *The Gambia–Senegal Border: Issues in Regional Integration.*

Routledge Studies in African Development

African Environmental Crisis
A History of Science for Development
Gufu Oba

Development in Nigeria
Promise on Hold?
Edlyne Eze Anugwom

Mineral Resource Governance and Human Development in Ghana
Felix Danso

Alternatives to Neoliberal Peace-Building and State-Building in Africa
Redie Bereketeab

Public Policy Lessons from the AIDS Response in Africa
Fred Eboko

Industrial Policy and the Transformation of the Colonial Economy in Africa
The Zambian Experience
Horman Chitonge

Responding to Mass Atrocities in Africa
Protection First and Justice Later
Raymond Kwun-Sun Lau

Politics in The Gambia and Guinea-Bissau
Precolonial Influence on the Postcolonial State
Mariama Khan

For more information about this series, please visit: www.routledge.com/Routledge-Studies-in-African-Development/book-series/RSAD

Politics in The Gambia and Guinea-Bissau

Precolonial Influence on the
Postcolonial State

Mariama Khan

R Routledge
Taylor & Francis Group

LONDON AND NEW YORK

First published 2022
by Routledge
2 Park Square, Milton Park, Abingdon, Oxon OX14 4RN

and by Routledge
605 Third Avenue, New York, NY 10158

Routledge is an imprint of the Taylor & Francis Group, an informa business

© 2022 Mariama Khan

British Library Cataloguing-in-Publication Data
A catalogue record for this book is available from the British Library

Library of Congress Cataloging-in-Publication Data
Names: Khan, Mariama, 1977– author.
Title: Politics in the Gambia and Guinea-Bissau : pre-colonial influence on the postcolonial state / Mariama Khan.
Description: Abingdon, Oxon ; New York, NY : Routledge, 2022. |
Series: Routledge studies in African development |
Includes bibliographical references and index. |
Identifiers: LCCN 2021041889 (print) | LCCN 2021041890 (ebook)
Subjects: LCSH: Gambia–Politics and government–21st century. |
Guinea Bissau–Politics and government–21st century. | Gambia–Social conditions–21st century. | Guinea Bissau–Social conditions–21st century.
Classification: LCC J741.G3 K43 2022 (print) |
LCC J741.G3 (ebook) | DDC 966.5103–dc23
LC record available at https://lccn.loc.gov/2021041889
LC ebook record available at https://lccn.loc.gov/2021041890

ISBN: 978-0-367-69005-2 (hbk)
ISBN: 978-0-367-69006-9 (pbk)
ISBN: 978-1-003-14000-9 (ebk)

DOI: 10.4324/9781003140009

Typeset in Times New Roman
by Newgen Publishing UK

Contents

Acknowledgments

I started writing this book in 2019 and presented parts of it at the 2nd Annual Mid-Atlantic and Great Lakes African Studies Conference at the University of Pittsburgh on 11 May 2019. Since then, I received excellent feedback from anonymous reviewers, whose comments and suggestions were invaluable in shaping the content of the book. I extend profound thanks to them. I would like to profoundly acknowledge and thank Helena Hurd and Rosie Anderson for their support with the book, and to Leila Walker for her help in the past. I thank Professor Peter Karibe Mendy, Professor Pierre Englebert, João Bernardo Vieira, Braima Sanhá and Malam Mané for sharing their insights on Guinea-Bissau with me. I also thank Sunkareh Jabang, Jainaba Kanyi, Mariama Camara, Ba Karamo Manneh, Demba Ceesay, Dr Adama Mbodj and Sulayman Sanyang for sharing their insights on Gambian politics. I extend special thanks to Dembo Kambi, my valuable research assistant. Additionally, I acknowledge Dr Mark Christian, my boyz Abdul, Omar and Muhammad, and brother Omar Khan.

Introduction
The search for good leadership

Lies have width but their length do not go far.

(Mandinka proverb)

If you do not know where you are going return to where you come from.

(Wollof proverb)

Political culture in postcolonial Gambia and Guinea-Bissau has been largely slippery and divisive. For many, politics mean to maneuver, wrench spoils from a struggling collective, and live large. This view sees politics as an amoral affair of the self-interested. It separates social morals and collective ethics from political culture. But political culture derives from society. Like a toxic body of water, divisive politics flows into the fabric of society to soak it deep with its polluted force. This is partly why politics in The Gambia and Guinea-Bissau has been beyond comprehension, full of unpredictable patterns and outcomes. In short, politics in the two countries is literally insane.

Widespread social disenchantment with immoral politics has given rise to what I call Justice, Integrity and Truth (JIT) movements in countries like Mali, Guinea-Bissau, The Gambia and Senegal. JIT is a pun derived from *nJit*, which means leader in Wollof. JITs are largely spearheaded by youths and women, and their influence has rapidly expanded since 2016. They demand civic or democratic leadership, moral politics, good and effective leadership; politics that sees "the nation" not sectionalist divisions, wipes out or lessons corruption and patrimonial practices. They mobilize people across regions, ethnicities, religions, etc. Thus, JITs are the rising oppositional force to the old way of doing politics in Africa. Senegal is one country in which they have made a prominent mark in the political and social scenes. From the President Abdoulaye Wade era Y'en Mare (from the French meaning

DOI: 10.4324/9781003140009-1

"Enough is Enough") movement to the Macky Sall era Nittu Degg (a Wollof term meaning "A Person of Truth") movement, the search for truth, justice, cultural dignity and moral politics is a defining call for JITs. Their renewed cultural awareness is highlighted as they employ indigenous terms, phrases and motifs to communicate their aspirations. Since JITs are more advanced and better developed in Senegal, I will draw enough examples from there.

This book studies the evolving nature of political rhetoric in The Gambia and Guinea-Bissau, two country cases that are often overlooked in scholarly conversations about the state in Africa. It uses oral traditions, indigenous songs, literature, interviews, newspaper and archival sources to demonstrate how cultural memory is appropriated to reveal the way traditional norms of statecraft are reclaimed, reinvented or subverted to create postcolonial political cultures and practices that meander between different historical epochs – precolonial and colonial. In The Gambia and Guinea-Bissau, people make references to Kaabu, a precolonial Mandinka empire to project their political and social visions. Large areas of both countries were part of the empire, which is a source of political rhetoric, ideas and practices among people from the two countries. Rhetoric is used to mean the art of influencing audiences by using arguments, emotions, character and other forms of persuasion. As a tool for social and political education, it shapes social practices and views (see Hauser, 2017). Some Gambians and Bissau-Guineans appropriate history and culture to project political visions in the quest for orderly politics, truthful leaders, and meaningful state practice and belonging.

Kaabu was founded by Mandinkas from the Mali empire, which was founded by Mande people. Kaabu, like Mali, was founded on strong Mande values and ethics, which include *Telingho* (justice or being just), *Forooya* (possessing an exemplary character), *Mooya* (endowed with social intelligence), *Hakiliyerewa* (consciousness, the source of wisdom and critical thinking) and *Sobeya* (values for hard work and seriousness). These values and ethics shaped Mandinka cultural and political philosophies and contributed to making them notable state-builders in West Africa. The ancestral pledge that honors "Manding suma fulo, anin ayere labangho" (the "first and last people of Manden") became the cornerstone of their state-building initiatives in West Africa. It is an integral part of modern Mandinka political and cultural ambitions. It is also the source of the cultural slogan "Mandinka faasa" (fighting for Mande values and culture or Mande-ness), which has become a mobilizing force for Gambians or Bissau-Guinean Mandinkas. Some Mandinkas appropriate the term in an exclusive sense. But traditionally it was used to mobilize and free Mandinka people from Susu domination and later for assimilating other non-Mandinka groups.

The book explores how latent but influential precolonial political traditions and practices are reclaimed, reinvented or subverted in modern-day Gambian and Bissau-Guinean politics. Its main research question is: how have certain precolonial political traditions and practices shaped politics in both The Gambia and Guinea-Bissau? This approach to studying the state will help us understand politics from top down to bottom up. It provides useful and generalizable ideas about new ways we can understand the state in Africa. More importantly, it highlights both the traditional and modern nature and measurements of leadership, power, authority, and followership in these two countries.

The main argument of the book is that in both The Gambia and Guinea-Bissau anti-colonial leaders effectively used culture and traditions to mobilize and successfully free their countries from colonial rule. But under the postcolonial state, their use of culture and other indigenous resources for organizing, executing and practicing the state degenerated. From the 1970s, most postcolonial African countries overlooked working on the state. Their attentions were diverted by dependence on exogenous expert ideas, servicing debt conditions and in responding to other external demands exerted on the state. These issues affected how the state sees and relates to society and vice-versa.

This book further argues and emphasizes that, at independence, most African leaders subcontracted thinking about the state to social scientists from the West. Due to the complexes they developed about the colonial model and its racial theories about the superiority of European culture over African culture, the new African bourgeois class did not adequately explore encoding the state within African thoughts to embed it in its rightful cultural foundation. The contemporary African state remains an illusion. Citizens did not develop social and cultural confidence in the state. They lack psychic or cognitive assurance in its legitimacy, security and dependability. As postcolonial rulers face "psychic turbulence" so do citizens who were or are not ideologically and philosophically incorporated within the state. The state fails to deliver to society tangible positive outcomes, like improved well-being, welfare, and better educational, health, and livelihood conditions, security and stability. Politics remains as an adventurist forage, not a conscious endeavor that must bring better livelihood outcomes for the broader society. The reclaiming, reproducing or subverting of traditional norms of power and authority in The Gambia and Guinea-Bissau is therefore influenced by a continuous search for a meaningful state, leadership, power, authority, and followership, all of which have repercussions for social reproduction and advancement in society.

These arguments are relevant to understanding JITs and their demands for an orderly political culture, truthful leaders and a just and equitable state that is responsive to the needs of citizens. The mission of JITs can be understood in relation to Ekeh's conclusion that "any politics without morality is destructive" (Ekeh, 1975: 111). Ayittey (2006) observed that at independence African nationalists should have retained what was positive in the colonial experience but shed off its negative effects. For example, peace and order should have been maintained at all costs, since both are vital for economic production and advancement. JITs demand such agency from African leaders and their followers. Agency is used here to mean

"directed, meaningful, intentional and self-reflective social action" (Chabal, 2009:7).

Bayart (2009) implied, and Chabal and Daloz (1999) stated, that disorder is functional to the African state. But demands for moral, ethical and results-oriented leadership indicate disorder is not natural to the African state. It is rather a symptomatic development that reflects complicated legacies of colonial and postcolonial experiences. Because as de Waal (2009) argued, political order was an important feature of many precolonial or premodern African states (see Chapter 1).

Notably, the creation of the Coordination of Movements, Associations and Sympathizers (Coordination des Mouvements, Association et Sympathisants, CMAS) in Mali, in September 2019, became a successful trendsetter for JITs. Founded by Imam Mahmoud Dicko, a politico-religious leader, the movement organized several demonstrations against President Ibrahim Boubacar Keita (IBK) of Mali in 2019 and 2020. In the end, a military coup d'état forced IBK to resign from power in August 2020. Imam Dicko surprised both national and international observers when he declined all positions in the post-IBK government led by Bah Ndaw. He declared he was an imam and would continue to be so. His decision is reminiscent of a practice in the Mali empire and among the Jahanke where religious authority provided spiritual and moral guidance to leadership and the population and largely abstained from coveting political power (see Sanneh 1979, 2016). This situation invokes the question: who has legitimacy to rule?

In 2016, Movimento dos Cidadaos Concientes e Inconformados (MCCI, the Non-Compliant Citizens Movement) was created in Guinea-Bissau to challenge the country's disorderly politics. According to João Bernardo Vieira, former Bissau-Guinean minister of transportation and infrastructure, the movement was made up of "Citizens who are conscious and not pleased about the current situation in Guinea-Bissau. Members staged protests against the former president, José Mário Vaz in 2016. Eventually, they left the country for exile."

In The Gambia, the political pressure group Operation 3-Years Jotna (which means in Wollof "three years is up") organized a protest against President Adama Barrow in December 2019. They demanded he resign after three years in power in line with the "gentleman's agreement" the coalition parties reached before they contested the 2016 elections. The group emerged as Barrow parted ways with his political godfather, the lawyer Ousnainou Darboe, leader of the United Democratic Party (UDP). Darboe served first as the coalition government's foreign minister and later vice president. But subsequently Barrow removed him from power. While in government, Darboe was in favor of the five-year mandate stated in the Gambian constitution, and not the coalition's three years transitional timetable. The bitter political divorce between Barrow and Darboe splintered UDP, the majority party in the coalition arrangement. Some members joined Barrow and advocated for the five-years mandate. Eventually, they formed a break-away party called the National People's Party (NPP) led by Barrow. To UDP followers, this was the ultimate betrayal. They began dispensing anti-Barrow rhetoric and branded the president *janfala* (meaning "betrayer" in Mandinka).

Barrow was sworn in as president in January 2017 after an intense political impasse that started in December 2016. When Alieu Momar Njie, the chairman of the Independent Electoral Commission, had to update the initial election results due to errors, Yahya Jammeh, the incumbent, contested the results of the elections after initially accepting them. The new results still gave Barrow the lead but with a wider margin over the incumbent. Jammeh and his party, the Alliance for Patriotic Reorientation and Construction (APRC), alleged there were irregularities in the results and asked for fresh elections. Subsequently, an international negotiation, which included the United Nations (UN), the Economic Community of West African States (ECOWAS) and some West African heads of states, saw Jammeh leave for Equatorial Guinea while Barrow was installed as president. The negotiation also included the deployment to The Gambia of a "peace-keeping" force, known as the ECOWAS Military Intervention group (ECOMIC), to "protect" Barrow. Since then, ECOMIC, which many observers see as a camouflage for Senegalese military presence in The Gambia, has been operating, but with significant controversies.

Barrow's coming to power was eagerly celebrated by many Gambians and international observers, with slogans such as "new Gambia," "Gambia has decided" and "democracy," etc. Since 2018, the bright outlooks toward the regime have largely darkened. The government, including its foreign service abroad, has been marred by both huge and petty corruption scandals. This was worsened by rising cost of living, a semi- dysfunctional public service, growing insecurity in the country, the growing number of murders of especially women, missing children, rampant street muggings, home burglaries and unexplained fires at public markets. Many self-styled political activists have also emerged under banners of civil society or religious or ethnic groups. Political discourse now largely consists of acerbic ethnic-based rhetoric. Daily, individuals or groups deploy and spread social media messages on morality, or in support of Barrow's government, or highlighting its failures, or promoting unhelpful ethnic rhetoric, among other topics.

The roles Gambians in the diaspora – largely from the USA, UK, Germany, Italy and Spain – continue to play in shaping political discourse in the country remain significant. Sometimes, these diaspora-based Gambians feel they have not been given the status most of them think they deserve in the "new Gambia." Feelings of entitlement amid the lackluster performance of Barrow's presidency made some of them present themselves as presidential hopefuls. As the December 2021 presidential election approaches, more than 18 political parties with some independent presidential candidates have announced they will contest the elections for a country of about two million people. Some of them question Barrow's moral bearing. However, some of the people have no better moral standing than him. For example, many Gambians received their residency status in Europe or USA through asylum applications. It is not uncommon for people to concoct stories about undergoing political persecution, which never happened to them to gain residency status in Europe or America. Some concoct other stories to get their way through. The combination of such acts has implications for social morality and truth-telling in society. This situation has forced many people to become "activists," especially during Jammeh's time, to feign some credibility to their status. In some cases, the moral scrutiny of Barrow presents a double-standard depending on who is gauging him.

As the fall-out between the NPP and UDP escalates, some political activists who were once former buddies, but are now estranged friends, have started revealing some ethically disturbing activities they engaged in during their "struggle" to unseat Jammeh. For example, some former UDP and diaspora-based Gambian activists confessed they paid people to burn down public places in The Gambia. The confessors also claimed they made up and staged stories that Jammeh was engaged in the ritual killing of babies, and was hosting Casamance rebels in The Gambia national army. Both allegations were proven false in the post-Jammeh era. Jammeh's arch-rival, President Macky Sall, also, who allegedly sold the same theories to the UN to get support for military intervention during the political impasse, could not prove the veracity of the allegations in the post-Jammeh era.

It further emerged that some diaspora-based Gambians also paid Solo Sandeng to "burn down" The Gambia. In the process, he lost his life.[1] Sandeng's case was one of the cases the Truth, Reconciliation and Reparation Commission (TRRC) investigated and on which they collected testimonies. The TRRC was set up by Barrow's government to investigate human rights abuses conducted under Jammeh's rule and it concluded its sittings around May 2021. The country now awaits its final report.

The moral double-standards in Barrow-era politics are further demonstrated when Alagie Saidy-Barrow, a former convicted criminal in the USA, was hired to be the chief investigator of the TRRC in The Gambia. However, anti-Jammeh activists argue that since the USA convicted him for trying to overthrew Jammeh, that does not disqualify him to work for the TRRC. They argue all strategies for removing him from power were "fair game." This attitude is similar to the miscalculated July 2021 proposal the diaspora-based Senegalese activists announced through their "ambassador" Kayz Fof, a social media political activist, that any Senegalese who can capture or get rid of President Macky Sall will be paid 200 million CFA francs, about 356,000 US dollars. Like the anti-Jammeh Gambians in the diaspora, these Senegalese are impatient to see Sall complete his mandated term, which ends in 2024. Additionally, they underestimate the kinds of risk this approach to getting rid of him can have on the security and stability of Senegal.

Importantly, these stories are about moral politics. But they also indicate questions about legitimacy for both leaders and followers. The way the diaspora-based populations of countries like The Gambia, Guinea-Bissau and Senegal try to influence political change in their countries can be partly understood in terms of Ekeh's (1975) idea of "psychic turbulence." The term denotes how educated Africans who inherited power from the colonizers realized they did not have moral authority to justify their rule to their people. Most of them were from non-chiefly backgrounds or families who did not enjoy traditional leadership authority. Ekeh uses the term "bourgeois" instead of "elite" to characterize them. He argued they lacked firm legitimacy. But as the only educated people at the time of independence, they had new privileged status. They can have lot of economic influence, but little political acceptance. They can wield power, but have little authority.

Diaspora-based populations of The Gambia, Guinea-Bissau and Senegal have significant economic influence due to the remittances they send back to their families at home. By virtue of their travel abroad, and sometimes their education, they feel they merit running the country and thus can instigate undemocratic changes of government to ensure they become leaders in their countries. However, most of them do not have the confidence to join the political process in the quest to become leaders. Many of them doubt their abilities to legitimately attract votes from the people. This resonates with Ekeh's view that Western education no longer suffices for political legitimacy in postcolonial Africa. The same is also true of traveling abroad and living in the "diaspora."

This mentality offers a good explanation of how, on 30 December, 2014, a group of Gambian mercenaries, mainly from the USA, attempted to overthrow Jammeh. They were funded by businessman Cherno Njie from Texas. Their ill-conceived strategy led to unnecessary loss of lives. To many observers, Njie and his co-conspirators' attempt to overthrow the government was a complete joke. They developed what is best described as a childish strategy for overthrowing Jammeh. They attacked the country but were repelled and vanquished by forces of The Gambia National Army. The surviving members, including Njie, were later tried and imprisoned in the USA. Under US law, Gambian law and in all decent laws of the world, these 30 December mercenaries are bona fide criminals. Two of them, Njie and Papa Faal, still want to become president in The Gambia. However, some people in the diaspora excuse their undemocratic attempt to depose an elected government. They call them "30 December heroes." This tag further exposes the moral inconsistency in the politics of Gambians in the diaspora. For example, some of the vocal critics who condemned Jammeh, and now Barrow, as corrupt, overlook their own past and sometimes continuing moral indiscretions, such as embezzling public funds, rape or abuse of women and so on. The use of meritless flowery terms to whitewash morally, legally or ethically questionable conduct resonates with Ekeh's view about the roles "ideologies" play in colonial and postcolonial African politics. By ideologies, he means the "unconscious distortions or perversions of truths by intellectuals in advancing points of views that favor or benefit the interests of particular groups for which the intellectual acts as spokesperson." They are part of the "invention of aesthetically appealing interest-begotten theories or ideologies, that detract from scientific truth" (Ekeh, 1975: 94). The abuse of truths, like ideological distortions, indicate insecurity among the people who promote those abused truths or ideologies. The Gambian and Bissau-Guinea diaspora disproportionately shape how such ideologies are propagated, spread and re-created to shape political views. Though their effects quickly erode with time.

However, it is important to note that not all people in the diaspora manipulate public opinion. There are many genuine and conscientious people in the diaspora. But most of the time you cannot find many of these people at the forefront of political activism. Notwithstanding, the tendency for the politically active part of the diaspora to have one rule for themselves and another rule for other people or leaders of the country further complicates politics in countries like The Gambia and Guinea-Bissau.

The moral double-standards in the politics of the diaspora can also be compared to the colonial and postcolonial politics of the home country where, in some cases, character is given secondary importance in the pursuit of political goals. It resonates with Chabal's observation that there has been a longstanding assumption that African politicians lack moral integrity. Hence, corruption continues to undermine the continent's development. This assumption is further reinforced with a race-based justification that "Politics in Africa lack morality, ... because African beliefs are obsolete," which implies "traditional" beliefs are not suited to the morality of the "modern world," (Chabal 2009: 67). But the emergence of JITs, most of which are reclaiming traditional African values to guide politics, indicates that, after more than half a century, most African countries have failed to deliver a fulfilling state which, since the colonial times, was largely guided by colonial moral architecture.

Ekeh's outstanding contribution to African politics justifies why JITs are pushing for the return to African morals and ethics to guide political culture and practice. He argued there are two publics in Africa, which operate on different moral foundations. The first one is the *primordial public* that is characterized by morality. People's membership of it is motivated by non-material incentives and personal sacrifices that require material and non-material investments to the causes of the primordial public. It values moral duties rather than the material worth of those duties. In other words, people give materially to the primordial public. But what they gain in return are not material but psychological benefits, such as emotional security or identity.

In contrast, the *civic public*, the second public, is amoral and is measured in material terms. Its tendencies dominate most parts of postcolonial African political culture and behavior. It embodies corrupt and patrimonial actions. It lacks generalized moral imperatives Therefore, leaders in the civic public use amoral strategies to secure their political leverage. Overall, conduct that is acceptable in the civic public can become scandalous in the primordial.

These two kinds of moral reservoirs determine what can or cannot be in associative life in most African countries. It connects to the idea of legitimacy. But before discussing it in detail, I establish what morality means in the context of the primordial public and JITs. As Chabal indicated, morality derives from "*religion, tradition* and *obligation.*" Its elements include virtuous behavior, accountable action and reciprocal influences. These values and ethical principles are being reclaimed by JITS, as evident in the examples I share below.

As the political wrangling intensified between the NPP and UDP, a movement of religious leaders in The Gambia emerged on social media. Sometimes, members of the group act in individual capacities by making and sharing social media messages on what they think is not right in the governance of the country. At times, these individuals do not seem to support any particular political party. Recently, some members called for *salatul layli* ("night prayers" in Islam) and mass giving out of assigned charities to rescue the country from its bad politics. They ask people to pray for God to give the country a good leader to lead it well.

The moral dilemmas they are speaking and praying against are determined by certain social moral parameters about honesty, virtue, public service and working in public interest-based work. They worry about falsehood and untruths that threaten public life. For example, as the December 2021 presidential elections approach in The Gambia, a video widely circulated on social media showed a sick person on a drip in a hospital bed, while a heavy downpour lashes the patient. The voice of an unidentified woman in the video claimed that Barrow's government was inhumanely treating even its sick citizens. The video was intended to show the brokenness of the Gambian health system. But when it was fact-checked, it emerged, according to Samsudeen Sarr, a Gambian writer, a former soldier, and an APRC supporter, and some NPP supporters, that the image was not from The Gambia. It was observed that there has not been such a heavy downpour in the country since the 2021 rainy season started. The intended manipulation of public opinion was caught early in its tracks and generally dismissed by many people.

Senegal also offers some interesting examples on how citizens react to the dubious manipulation of public opinion in order to advance political goals or damage political opponents. In the recent political crisis in the country, a supporter of the ruling party used voice-cloning technology and recorded an audio message calling for violent political insurgence, in the name of Nitt Doff, a Senegalese activist. He also created a Facebook page in his name to spread seditious messages. However, the dubious plot backfired. Senegalese were stunned by the extent the man had gone to falsely incriminate Doff. But such political manipulations have become ever more common in the politics of countries like The

Gambia, Guinea-Bissau and Senegal, especially with the access some state agents and some oppositional forces have to deepfake technology (see Chapter 3).

Since March 2021, Macky Sall continues to be confronted by massive opposition and protests from Senegalese citizens in the country and the diaspora. They forcefully oppose his plans for a *troism mandate* (a third term/mandate) for the 2024 elections. They demand that he keep his promise to stand for two terms only. Moreover, they claim that he has betrayed Senegal, embezzles its resources, plots to destroy political opponents, leads a government of conspirators, governs with "darkness" and has no respect for Senegalese values and traditions. Ousmane Sonko, the 46-year-old leader of PASTEF, currently the most popular opposition party in the country, has emerged as the symbol of what many Senegalese call "cutting-off the rope of enslavement," protecting "Senegalese uprightness," "freedom," "modesty" and "Senegalese interests." They hail him as the prospective architect of a Senegal that works for all Senegalese. The Movement of Young Marabouts of Medina Baye, an anti-Macky Sall group from Kaolack, a major Senegalese town, engages in prayers for Sonko and also makes financial contributions to his PASTEF party. There have been many other religious groups or individuals who have become self-declared supporters of Sonko. Later I will explore how he is already enjoying legitimacy as Sall's political fortunes deteriorate even in his native home territory of Fouta. But, before that, I want to explore the meaning and understanding of legitimacy in The Gambia and Guinea-Bissau, while using the political crisis in Senegal as lessons that reinforce the importance of moral debates in Gambian and Bissau-Guinean politics.

The first part of this chapter is the introduction. The next section explores the status of legitimacy and morality in African politics, with examples taken from The Gambia, Guinea-Bissau and other countries. This is followed by a brief discussion of political legitimacy in Kaabu and its relevance to present-day politics in The Gambia and Guinea-Bissau, with additional examples from Senegal. Then, a brief survey of the theories of the African state follows, after which I briefly discuss viewing the state from below through how it is represented in political oral arts. This is followed by a discussion of the colonial history, after which the methodology and the conclusion follow.

Legitimacy and morality

Ekeh (1975) argued that in Africa traditional kingship and chieftaincy were defined in moral terms. People who ruled had authority and their leadership models had indigenous cultural roots. European colonizers invented colonial ideologies to convince Africans that colonial rule was good for them. Subsequently, colonization created a new bourgeois class of Africans with Western education. The colonial state that was created "was Janus-faced, bifurcated. It consisted of dual forms of power under a single hegemonic authority. Urban power spoke the language of civil society and civil rights, rural power of community and culture" (Mamdani, 2018: 18). Ekeh noted the colonial struggle was about the clash between the colonizer and this new class of Africans, who depended on colonialism for their legitimacy. They accepted the principles of colonialism but rejected the foreign personnel who ruled them. They developed counter-ideologies to justify their competence to rule their people based on their Western education, since they lacked traditional authority. As such "African bourgeois ideologies of legitimation" created rulers who, like the European colonial rulers, do not readily fit within the social stratification system of the people they ruled or now rule. Unlike the defeated traditional aristocracy whose bases of power were weakened by the adoption of foreign techniques of governance, the new African bourgeois, in contrast to proper elites, became men who did not have autonomy in the formation of their values. Their decision-making processes were not independent of external sources. Over time, as the emergent African bourgeois class's legitimacy was threatened and they became insecure, they resorted to ethnic-based politics, borrowed from the colonial book of politics. Consequently, colonial thinking and practice shaped African postcolonial techniques of governance and statehood.

Migdal argues that when third world societies gained independence from colonial rule, there was much anticipation about the state's capacity to develop as African states were encoded in the cultural artifact of their former masters. The social sciences and Western social scientists of the 1950s and 1960s provided the new African rulers with ideological blueprints for running the new African states. But over time these prescriptions, which yielded significant undesirable results for African political growth and development, became "intertwined with the professional failures of social scientists" (Migdal, 1988: 10–11). In other words what Englebert (2000) called the "insight outside quality of the state" impedes political advancement in most African countries. In the absence of African thinking, the unified vision of the state has been difficult to achieve.

Since this book is about statecraft, I define how the following terms have been used in the work. Statecraft is the art of creating different institutions, codes of ethics and practice rules for leaders and followers. These systems work cohesively in service to citizens or subjects of the state to achieve the stated or perceived ideals of a state. Politics means here "everything from institutions to mass behaviour" (Olson, 2011: 640). Political culture means the set of patterns, principles and practices of governance that can be traced as specific to a particular people or polity in the long durée. Customs is defined as "a set of norms and conventions that regulated gender and generational relations" (Mamdani, 2018: xvi). Power means the ability to exercise agency to achieve one's goals. It can come from various sources, such as skills, attitude and character, social ascription, monopoly of force, or cooperative goodwill. Social norm means what is considered acceptable in the mind of the collective. It conforms to general social behavior, perceptions, customs and represent actions or perceptions that society is generally comfortable with. Political authority is defined as the decision of subjects to invest their trust in an actor in their society to mediate self-interested and collective needs to ensure that the common good is pursued and attained for a balanced and stable society. Social contract means an agreement between the governed and the governors that ensures the latter uses power, authority and public resources to pursue the interests of the governed through necessary social and political arrangements. It establishes law, order and security, creates public services, protects public morality and social cohesion/harmony. Public consent means when subjects or citizens recognize that the state is working to achieve and protect their interests, such as basic security, law and order, health, education, and other public services for an agreeable social life. This consent confers legitimacy to the state. Where necessary, other terms used in the rest of the book will also be clarified.

This book uses communitarian theories that center African politics within "Africa's age-old communities." It also revisits how modernist approaches to African politics foster a "liberal solution" that "locates politics in civil society" and the consequences this has in countries like The Gambia and Guinea-Bissau (see Mamdani, 2018, 3). The issue of state legitimacy is therefore a critical concern here. It takes its cue from Pierre Englebert's (2000) groundbreaking study of historical state legitimacy and its links to economic growth in Africa. However, like Mamdani, I focus more on culture and history, instead of the economy.

I argue that legitimacy is a revolving notion. It emanates from two main sources: firstly, the reclaiming or claiming the right to rule based on past ancestral association with cultural and historical sources of leadership; secondly, evolutionary legitimacy, which has two aspects. Individuals who had no previous hereditary references to leadership in their background can later find themselves in leadership ambits due to changes in society and new skills they have acquired. This resonates with Ekeh's description of the emergent African bourgeois class who inherited power from the colonizer thanks to their Western education and exposure to Western governmental techniques. The second aspect of evolutionary leadership involves the leader's ability to appeal to new sources of political authority hitherto excluded from political mainstreams, such as women and youth. Both leaders who have ancestral claims to leadership, and those that newly acquired leadership, must seek an evolutionary legitimization program for political or leadership success.

Leaders who reclaim their heritage and association with traditional authority to boost their leadership appeal to Weber's idea of traditional legitimacy. For example, The Gambia's former president, Yahya Jammeh, claims to be a descendant of Mama Tamba Jammeh, a legendary Baddibu *mansa*. Baddibu is located in the north bank region of The Gambia. It has a rich oral tradition. "Mama Tamba," a traditional musical composition, was composed in honor of Mama Tamba Jammeh and is part of the country's popular traditional beats. The song was appropriated under Jammeh's rule and served as an accompanying tune during inspections of guards of honor and other presidential functions (see Chapter 3). This was the background to the futile campaign some Jammeh supporters launched to crown him king of The Gambia during his presidency.

Dembo Fatty, a knowledgeable Gambian historian and authority in Gambian and Manden histories, argued to skeptics who doubt Jammeh–Mama Tamba connections that he can have ancestral links to the king. A political rift in Baddibu caused some members of Mama Tamba's family to flee to Foni, President Jammeh's ancestral region. For Fatty, this could be the source of the connection between the two Jammehs.

The late Bissau-Guinean military and political leader, General Ansumana Mané, was born in The Gambia but became a leader in Guinea-Bissau. His descent from the *nyanchoo*, the royal house or ruling class of Kaabu, reinforced his leadership. For many, his extraordinary military skills and political leadership was in his blood. Mané was embroiled in Guinea-Bissau's 1998 political crisis and was subsequently killed. However, there is a repertoire of musical compositions that celebrates his leadership, military service and even his poise, which was described as a royal, and charismatic resemblance of true *nyanchoo* royals (see Chapter 3). Umaro Sissoco Embaló, the current president of Guinea-Bissau, wears the *naaw*, a traditional head wrap bestowed on individuals who distinguished themselves as erudite and exceptional leaders in Mandinka and Fulani cultures. It also denotes a person of exceptional character and ethical conduct. Symbolically, Embaló's use of the *naaw* legitimizes him as someone with hereditary association to great learning, leadership and exemplary character and conduct (see Chapter 3). Thus, he uses history and culture to brand himself for better political acceptance.

Leaders who did not readily connect to traditional forms of authority are wont to employ "African bourgeois ideologies of legitimation" to promote their right to rule. In The Gambia, UDP supporters deride President Barrow, who was called an "accidental president" by a French journalist, for not having any ancestral claims to leadership. His opponents argue his government has "failed" because leadership is strange to him. They pit him against Lawyer Darboe, who they say has ancestral claim to religious leadership and is a descendant of a notable *wali* (saint) in Islam. In response to his detractors, Barrow calls himself the "bus driver" who can get people off the bus, an indirect reference to his firing of Darboe and other UDP officials in his government. However, his use of the bus as a political metaphor was seized on to further disparage his legitimacy. His critics conclude the bus is on a wild ride and has no direction. Hence, the "new Gambia" slogan adopted in the euphoria of Barrow's coming to power is now replaced with a Wollof one "*Gambia du dem*," (meaning "Gambia will not go"). It denotes a failed government. In response to frustrations about national security, Barrow tells Gambians he is in charge of the Gambian national army, the police and sub-regional ECOMIG forces that were deployed and are still present in the country following the 2017 political impasse (see Khan, 2019).

In Senegal, as Macky Sall's support dwindles rapidly, more and more Senegalese activists are using ancestral arguments on social media to denounce his leadership. Large numbers of youth and other Senegalese in the diaspora have rallied around his main opponent Ousmane Sonko's vision for a just, free, and developed Senegal, which has a strong pan-African ethos. In the eyes of many Senegalese, Sonko's appealing political vision, his character, virtues and heritage as a descendant of families with a history of exceptional religious and political leadership, makes him the right ruler for Senegal. Sonko is projected as the moral candidate discussed in the advice of Thierno Sulayman Bal, an 18th-century religious and political leader of Fouta Toro. He advised people should choose a leader "who is not interested in [the riches of] this world; and if you see that his possessions increase, depose him ... Bring to power one who deserves it, one who forbids his soldiers to kill defenseless children and old people, and to [rape] women, let alone kill them."

The moral discourses in Senegalese politics favor merit-based leadership. They sometimes wade into the ancestral origins of leaders to snub misperforming leaders using their heritage. These new moral discourses are also expressed in terms of "cutting off the rope of enslavement" ("duc bome jam" in Wollof) in Senegal, using Senegalese resources for Senegalese, and restrengthening democracy. The discourses appropriate memories of religious leaders like Cheikh Ahmadou Bamba (of the Mourid brotherhood), El Haj Malik Sy (of the Tijaniya), Bai Ibrahima Niass (of the Niassen), Seydina Limamou Laye (of the Layene) and political leaders like Mamadou Dia and Cheikh Anta Diop. Their memories and the memories of traditional leaders like Thierno Sulayman Bal constitute the icons for the "revolution" Senegalese are calling for. They believe Dia, the first prime minister of Senegal, was imprisoned by Leopold Sedar Senghor, Senegal's first president, based on a false allegation that he had attempted a coup d'état in 1962. The reclaiming of the past involves the reclaiming of various discourses about honor, collective security, justice, integrity and truth, which are termed the cornerstone for a workable fair and just Senegalese democracy. Political legitimacy is therefore being associated with traditional measurements of leadership, which demand knowledgeable leadership, leading for the people, responsiveness to their needs, honesty, trustworthiness, and protective action-orientedness. However, these values resonate with modern development and governance discourses.

Irrespective of the level of traditional legitimacy a leader enjoys, political expediency requires drawing on evolutionary legitimacy. This form of legitimacy evolves as a leader recognizes and appeals to "remodeled" power bases, which are not fixed but keep changing as society progresses. For example, President Museveni of Uganda raps to appeal to Ugandan youths, who also constitute the support base of his main political challenger Bobi Wine. Interestingly, Wine is a popular musician. By rapping and having a strong presence on social media, Museveni taps into "new" avenues to legitimize his rule and appeal to an expanding power base like the youth. President George Weah of Liberia has creatively used music to trash his political rivals. His single "Mr Liar Man," released in December 2020, is also an important legitimizing instrument.

The notion of evolutionary legitimacy is premised on an understanding that power structures shift continuously as political processes evolve. New strategies are employed to appeal to new power bases. Therefore, evolutionary legitimacy hardly has time to develop and loyally appeal to new sources of power. It is a politically expedient notion that is dependent on rotating power dynamics. Consequently, it is proactive, intuitive and counter-intuitive. The sources and meanings of power and authority can change to reflect new developments such as technological advancement (e.g. social media), demographic changes (the growth of diaspora populations), economic situations and external threats to the nation. This is evident in how Kabunka (the term used to refer to the people of Kaabu) social and political philosophies are reclaimed, appropriated or subverted in modern Gambian and Bissau-Guinean politics and social life. Other members of society also find themselves, albeit, at grassroots or lower levels of societal interactions, consciously or unconsciously driven by the search for legitimacy. The same applies to new elite political actors aiming to squeeze themselves within the now over-crowded and jammed political field in The Gambia and Guinea-Bissau. The next section introduces the nature of legitimacy in Kaabu's politics.

Kabunka political legitimacy and the present

The Gambia and Guinea-Bissau were both part of the Kaabu empire, which existed from 1537 to 1867 (see Chapter 1). Historically, the populations of the two countries shared a common culture and an international political economy, local and regional communications and trade networks. Their peoples are defined by close ties, similar ways of economic production, identical cultural forms and regional and international diplomatic policies (Colvin, 1975: 215–216).

There has been a longstanding practice in which people in colonial and postcolonial Gambia and Guinea-Bissau re-create, reclaim or subvert relevant oral histories, traditional motifs of power and authority from Kabunka politics or general Mandinka political thought. Therefore, this book reconstructs relevant aspects of Kaabu's political history to show how thoughts and practices from the empire continue to influence ideas of power, authority and politics in The Gambia and Guinea-Bissau.

The Kabunka leader whose rule offers relevant evidence for the arguments of this book, given the page limitation, is Mama Janky Wally, the last *mansa* or emperor of Kaabu. His reign embodied major innovations in the politics of the empire. His rule also coincided with colonial contact and the domination of African territories. Kaabu had its own systems for negotiating power and authority, mobilizing political consent, and ensuring inclusion, pillars for a stable, inclusive and accountable polity. Like any form of mass human organization, it had its crisis moments and forms of internal competition. However, there was shared understanding of what Kaabu meant and was to every Kabunka ruler and follower.

In Kaabu, the test of legitimacy was central to the *daal* ritual, where a king's appeal to the general populace is highlighted. *Daal* was an assessment of a ruler's truthfulness, his/her ability to communicate realizable political visions, and good judgment skills. Legitimacy was therefore the concessionary fabric of power and authority. It strengthens the voice and the image of the leader, and sows confidence in followers. Actionable power is therefore contingent upon solid legitimacy, which develops and grows over time (see Chapter 1).

Kaabu's political economy revolved around *nyanchoo* culture, a reinvention of the Mali empire's justice, knowledge and development-oriented political tradition founded under Sundiata Keita, and enshrined in the Manden charter of 1236. Oral arts played significant roles in Kabunka politics. *Nyanchoo* culture is examined in relation to five Mandinka political and social principles namely: *Telingho* (Justice/ or being just), *Forooya* (exemplary character), *Mooya* (social intelligence), *Hakiliyerewa* (consciousness, wisdom) and *Sobeya* (hard work and seriousness). These ideas are core to Mandinka philosophies on how societies grow, progress and decline. They are also relevant to the collapse of the Kaabu empire after its long existence as a vassal state of the Mali empire and later as an independent polity.

Ellis and Haar (1998) rightly predicted that, as political institutions break down in many African countries, new preoccupations about how power is organized will arise. The need for new systems can spur the revival of religious movements, as large sections of society question how power is acquired or distributed in society. This is in a context in which hitherto third world African countries continue to operate within institutions imposed on them through Western colonization. Debates about immorality of political systems and the need for reform continue to shape developments in the Senegalese political crisis. The political demands JIT movements are making on governments in West Africa are in no way side-stepping democracy. They imply legitimate power is inclusive, takes care of minorities and the weak, and is rotated in society. For example, Senegal's Collectif Noo Lank (which means in Wollof "we the collective resist") demands politics based on principles, visions and values. The opinions it represents include those from civil society, the opposition parties and other anti-government groups in Senegal. Their demands are influenced by indigenous measurements of good leadership. They appeal for new conceptions for legitimizing power to reconstruct the relevant apparatus for fulfilling the functions of government. Thus, President Sall, whose leadership skills and strategies are now widely questioned by Senegalese, found himself besieged by even his own traditional homeland. Below I explore how the recent political crisis involving Agi Sarr expanded demands for honest, truthful and moral politics in Senegal. In other words, the word must matter but so too must character.

In a video interview produced by a Senegalese online platform, Bambey TV, Abdourahman Ndiaye, youth leader and spokesperson of the collective of youths from Fouta, whose slogan is "Fouta Tampi" (which means that Fouta is exhausted or tired), declared:

> from the revolution of Thierno Sulayman Baal to date, the region of Fouta fully participated alongside the rest of Senegal to fight for the country ... we have all seen how the corona virus is ravaging the country ... but government officials come to Fouta to seek solidarity for Macky Sall because he is lonely in the current political crisis.

Ndiaye condemned the government-sponsored "mega meeting," which intended to mobilize support for Sall. "If Macky has become isolated, it is his own doing ... youth of Fouta have joined the rest of Senegal to protest against his government, we will not encourage sectionalism" (Fouta Tampi, 2021).

Fouta Toro (Fouta in short form) is located in northeastern Senegal. It is the ancestral home of the Tukulor (also spelt Toucouleur) people, the ethnic group President Macky Sall hails from. The region was, during past good times, dubbed his political "title deed." But Fouta has come to denounce its own even as some Senegalese activists condemn Sall's government for pushing ethnic politics on Senegal. Traditionally, the term "nedokubandun" has been an important ethnic mobilizing force among the Tukulor. It has similar conceptual standing to "Mandinkaya faasa." But the Fouta Tampi movement denounces "nedokubandun," upsetting Sall's political future.

Fatoumata Ndiaye, a Tukulour young woman and former close political associate of Sall's party, is the leader of the Fouta Tampi movement. By May 2021, she had received death threats from people believed to be supporters of the Sall regime. She went into hiding but re-emerged even more defiant. In her public interviews about her ordeals, she declared she was willing to be killed fighting for justice for Fouta and for Senegal. By June 2021, as a series of protests were organized against Sall, Senegalese adopted "Senegal Tampi" as a nationwide slogan to denounce him and his regime.

Ndiaye was not the only woman recently catapulted to national attention in Senegalese politics. In early February 2021, PASTEF's Ousmane Sonko was accused of rape by Adji Sarr, a young woman who worked in a massage parlor. Sonko denied the allegation and said it was politically motivated. He was arrested and detained by the government. Massive riots broke out all over Senegal demanding he must be freed. Other pro-Sonko demonstrations were held by Senegalese in France, Spain, the USA and in other countries around the world. The government released him.

On 8 March 2021, Idrissa Seck, a former leader of the opposition who joined the Sall government, publicly challenged Sonko to swear before the nation that he was innocent of the rape accusation. Sonko abided and swore before the nation. On 17 March 2021, Adji Sarr conducted an extensive but discomforting interview with the press, coached by El Haj Diouf, a controversial lawyer-politician. But during the interview, she was dressed in an Islamic veil for the first time in public. Many Senegalese condemned the staging as a political ploy to coerce public sympathy.

During the interview, Sarr cast aside the rape allegation, but maintained she had a relationship with Sonko. She also changed her previous plea that the latter threatened her with a gun before raping her. She challenged that if Sonko denied their relationship, he should perform an Islamic ritual birth and swear using the Qu'ran, the Islamic holy book. She would then withdraw her rape court case against him. She disclosed she was pregnant, but would give no further details about it. By the end of the interview, many observers suspected that Adji Sarr was a victim of Senegalese politics. In June 2021, the Senegalese minister of justice further dented her rape claim when he responded in a media interview that there was no rape, but admitted Sonko had a relationship with Sarr.

As the story of the rape allegation unfolded in its early phase, many Senegalese feminist organizations declared their support for Sonko. They too believed it was an ugly political set-up, executed in a woefully immature way. Sonko's public swearing further cemented the support he received across Senegal. Capitaine Oumar Toure, the chief investigator responsible for the rape investigation, resigned from his job in moral protest against political intrigue. Later, Sonko announced he had completely forgiven Sarr for the false allegation levelled against him. But that did not change the profound social condemnation she received in Senegal.

Sonko, who has become a subject of numerous songs composed to celebrate him by different Senegalese musicians, is seen by many as an embodiment of honest and patriotic leadership and a reincarnation of the great African leadership eliminated in colonial or neocolonial conspiracies. They equate him with Mamadou Dia, Cheikh Anta Diop,

Thomas Sankara and Patrice Lumumba. They make pledges to protect him. During protests, or group meetings, or Facebook live broadcasts, pro-Sonko supporters chant a Wollof anti-bullying traditional song, the words of which mean "if you touch him, I will beat you up." Sonko-themed adaptations of traditional songs are sung side by side with songs denouncing Sall, whose government attained notoriety when it successively tried and imprisoned two major political rivals, Khalifa Ababacar Sall and Karim Wade, on what were regarded as fabricated charges.

While Fatoumata Ndiaye is regarded a heroine in Senegal, and even if temporarily, as she subsequently recapitulated on her position. Senegalese media and some activists like Ousmane Tounkara and Mister Shake alleged she was bribed, some claim with two cars, two proper-ties and a hefty sum of money by the Sall government. Aji Sarr has become a derided villain. A woman from a vulnerable background has been caught up in a serious political in-fight. She was taken by the state and put under the custody of state forces and isolated from her family, who later demanded her release and return to them. Her father publicly apologized to Senegal and Sonko, and for the loss of lives during the pro-Sonko demonstrations. Sarr is a victim of Senegalese politics. She needs support and understanding. However, the political climate is not allowing that to happen.

Fatoumata Ndiaye and Aji Sarr's stories are different. But both fit moral discourses about truth-telling, whose words are more trust-worthy, and valuing truth and character above all other considerations like gender, ethnic or regional affiliation. The two stories are similar in the way they represent how women are politically abused or silenced, intimidated or used as pawns or sacrifices. Sarr's body was made into a political tool and her naivety was exploited in an attempt to damage and get rid of a political opponent, who many Senegalese regarded as clean, decent and dignified. As time passes and more truths are revealed, even from the government's end, she is becoming more and more isolated while people who recruited her for the "deal" receive partial public con-demnation. Her story resonates with recent trends in Gambian and Bissau-Guinean politics in which women are used to ensnare polit-ical rivals. The use of naked bodies as political tools and strategies for intimidating or infiltrating political rivals is not new. It takes its cue from the Atlantic slave trade and colonial rule. In postcolonial Gambia, it was a tool used following the 1981 rebellion organized by Kukoi Samba Sanyang. The later parts of the Jawara regime were allegedly notorious for similar abuses of women, who became sex assets exploited by high-ranking officials of the regime, in return for state benefits such as jobs, scholarships and so on. But it has become a hot political tool in post-Jammeh Gambia, in Guinea-Bissau and in Senegal.

Following the 1998 civil war in Guinea-Bissau, naked body politics was used to desecrate dead bodies. The general intent of such strategies is to humiliate, intimidate, or erode the dignity and humanity of victims. It defies human decency. It violates a protected and entrenched clause of the Kourukan Fouga, the constitution of the Mali empire, which stated the enemy could be killed, but never humiliated (see Chapters 1 and 2). The expanding popularity of naked body politics, like the use of public swearing, indicate the new pressures that politicians are facing in the midst of dwindling public trust. The use of public swearing rituals to ascertain innocence has been a longstanding traditional and customary practice in Kaabu and the Senegambia region. A person who falsely takes the oath invokes a curse on himself/herself. Public swearing was therefore an important social and political tool for deterring liars, establishing truth and truthfulness (see Chapter 1). The call for Sonko's public swearing as a form of declaring his innocence in the rape allegation also has Islamic sanctions. Some verses in Surah 24 of the holy Qu'ran (Al-Nuur) command that if someone accuses another person of adultery or fornication on the basis of uncorroborated solitary evidence, the accuser should take an oath and invoke a curse on himself/herself to prove he/she is telling the truth. The use of religiously-sanctioned or cultural moral codes and ethical value systems are ever more becoming integrated in political discourses, especially during crisis.

In religious and cultural circles, lying under oath is believed to result in *halakoo* (Mandinka), or *h'alak* (Wollof), a curse, which in Senegambia religious beliefs has devastating consequences and never fails to catch up with defaulters. But depending on the moral convictions of the oath taker, some people do still lie under oath. Some observers of the testimonies that happened under The Gambia's TRRC concluded that some of the witnesses whose testimonies under oath clearly indicated they were lying and fabricating evidence were doing themselves a disservice, given *halakoo* would later catch up with them. However, the TRRC's swearing of witnesses follows modern judicial traditions. Nevertheless, the use of cultural and religious sanctioned public swearing codes in public discourses also indicates people's lack of faith in the formal justice system.

The political abuse of women is also connected to the abuse of youths by tempting, forcing or intimidating them with alcoholism, drug use and other forms of delinquent behavior. McGhee argues that youth are important agents for organizing and reproducing social and political life. International NGOs have used selections of African youths as the "purported fount of moral reform across the continent." Cherry-picked youth who gain "surrogate membership in the affluent echelons of a middle-class African diaspora" experience new forms of isolation from their African cultural ties. They constitute new concerns as they evolve in the "refigured moral politics of time and tradition" international NGOs are building for African communities as part of "newly transformative regimes of hope, morality and futurity" (McGee, 2019: 170). This implies the grooming of different categories of youth in society. But any sustainable future for any African country must include building broad shared visions among all the youth, visions embedded in African cultural and social thoughts. While some youth become project models for certain external moral visions, others are used as weapons for political battles. The abuse of youth for political aims can include the instigating of children against parents perceived as political opponents. This is part of a broad politics of fabrication and betrayal in which not only youths but also women and families are divided against one another through the use of various forms of political intrigue to intimidate or blackmail political opponents (see Chapter 3).

During a UDP press conference on 3 July 2021 on Kerr Fatou, a TV program in The Gambia, lawyer Ousainou Darboe declared in Mandinka that those who are defaming him can go ahead. He will not share the ugly things he knows about them. However, it is the family members of those defamers who will denigrate them, not him. Prior to this press conference, Baba Jah (Ebou Bah), an NPP supporter who is from Brikama but lives in Seattle, USA, conducted a controversial TV interview on Darboe. Bah, who said he was a former close youth associate of Darboe, revealed some dark activities he alleged were conducted by Darboe. Some political observers saw the interview as part of the ongoing NPP–UDP feud.

Before the press conference and interview, Barrow had a meeting with *alkalos* and chiefs in the West Coast region, which was also broadcast on 3 July 2021 by an online TV platform called Gambia Political Zone. He denounced what he considered the UDP's tribe- and thug-based politics. He also disclosed that Dr Sedat Jobe, a senior member of the UDP, led a UDP delegation to the office of the Senegalese ambassador in The Gambia to demand that Senegal respect The Gambia's sovereignty and stop interfering in Gambian politics (Gambia Political Zone, 2021). The "ECOMIC" presence in The Gambia, which is seen as a camouflage for Senegalese military occupation, has seen its own fair share of controversies, ignited sometimes by the conduct of individual personnel or by the perceived excesses Senegalese soldiers exert on Gambians in the country. The general social insecurity that exists under

Barrow is also understood in terms of mortgaging the country's sovereignty to Senegal. UDP has condemned this. NPP supporters and other Gambians claim that UDP is aiming to plunge The Gambia into civil war, which UDP denies. Bah's interview further alleged a fetishist from India consulted by Darboe in his presence told him that if he becomes a leader the country will be chaotic. His interview was the climax of the most recent feuds between the two parties.

Importantly, it captures some of the ways politics has been done in countries like The Gambia and Guinea- Bissau. The way individuals in the diaspora become influential but controversial political players brings to mind how national and transnational politics shape each other. It also indicates the involvement of external political influences or influencers that shape politics in some contexts.

In Senegal, Macky Sall has the uncommon fate of having three people who have the same first names, Ousmane, as his major political nemesis. They are Ousmane Ba, an activist in Canada, Ousmane Tounkara, an activist in New Jersey and Ousmane Sonko, the leader of PASTEF. Ba, Tunkara, Kayz Fof and Akthenaton (two other activists in, it appears, France) feed social media with what could sometimes be considered classified information on the Sall regime and its activities. For example, recently, Ba went online and provided his viewers with direct phone numbers for President Sall and some members of his government. He also shared phone communication transcripts of two important government officials. This action brings to mind the various forms of moral templates that inform political activism in West Africa. But activism in the diaspora takes its cue from national level organizing. For example, *Ande Sameu Djiko Yi* (which means in Wollof "together to protect values") has emerged as another powerful organizing platform in Senegal. It is a coalition of 50 Senegalese organizations. They claim their goal is to protect Senegalese cultural and religious values. One of the unique characteristics of contemporary political organizing is the use of religious motifs, indigenous languages and traditional musical or folklore symbols.

Ellis and Haar (1998) observe that widespread religious trends embodied by Islamic renewal and Pentecostal revival movements have political significance in Africa. With deep-rooted intermingling of religion and politics, such movements evolve when, or as, institutions of the state rot away. The authors argue such movements are premised on combating evil and rooting out perceived impurities that give rise to witch-finding missions and similar witchcraft-related debates and activities (see Chapter 3). They visibly occupy public space, conduct public ceremonies and parades as precursors of spiritual and political stability. Their role in postcolonial politics is emblematic of precolonial African politics, where state religious performances were important parts of the political system. Some of their members play roles as ritual experts who can mediate between the visible and invisible worlds to achieve political, social and spiritual goals. Ellis and Haar further note that religious communities become sources of votes, creating clienteles or organizing constituencies for politicians. In most African societies people believe the ultimate source of power is the invisible world. Therefore, discourses about power are invariably connected to discourses about morality. The people believe the roles of ritual experts, as spiritual guarantors of power places them within an "exclusive moral realm." Religious movements attempt to locate new sources of power to provide social cohesion and can therefore challenge the legitimacy of the state or a leader. It is within this context that different socio-religious groups are becoming important political voices and organizing platforms in The Gambia, Guinea-Bissau, Senegal and Mali.

The search for truthful leaders has shaped political discourses about morality at a time when ever more people are no longer attracted to post-truth politics or political deception from leaders. The role youth is playing in JIT movements is shaped by cultural awareness but also the realization of the existence of a corps of youth or leaders who are groomed or being groomed in opposition to broader society's aspirations.

Another dimension of abusive politics is the use of what I called the *maruf* strategy to eliminate real or perceived political rivals. The word *maruf* derives from *marufu*, a Mandinka religious term that signifies how Satan came to Adam and Eve on a pretext of friendship but deceived them and caused their expulsion from heaven. The term is also used to describe a deceitful, scheming individual in society. The *maruf* strategy has two parts: first, it involves overt overtures of friendship in order to penetrate political targets, get their trust, know their weaknesses and then use those to strike against them to eliminate, blackmail or intimidate them politically. Its second aspect uses symbols or motives from rival political actors, party or groups to harass, intimidate or plot against other political targets by diverting their attention from the real perpetrator(s) of those political maneuvers. This employs psychological tactics to sow distrust between a political target and his/her allies by deceptively adopting motives or symbols associated with those allies to execute political intrigues against the target. This has become a commonly used political strategy in social media-based politicking as well as in day-to-day political maneuvers outside social media. The next section explores how theories of the African state interact with culture and history to shape views of the state.

The African state in theory: power of culture and history

Chabal (2009) stated that there have been about seven main theoretical frameworks for analyzing and debating postcolonial African politics. These are "development, Marxist, dependency, socialist, indigenous, neo-patrimonial and democratic" theories about the state (Chabal, 2009: 3). Development theory expounds the assumptions that there is a defined path for economic development and countries must follow that. Secondly, Africa can be jump-started to catch up with the developed world. Marxists or neo-Marxists share a similar conviction but unlike development theory, both believe that socialism and the one-party system, not capitalism and competitive politics, should drive political and economic progress. Like the socialist theory, they seek to regulate Africa's dependence on the world market and global capitalist economic systems. Indigenous theories capture the spirit of local rather than universal conceptualizations of African politics. They embrace Afrocentric perspectives that refocus history and the social sciences as they question the validity of both modernization and Westernization. Neo-patrimonial theories make two key arguments – that the transplanted Western state has failed to embed in Africa and that African politics reflects patrimonial cultures of their specific contexts. Democratic theory is influenced by institutional notions of political change. Liberal democracy is therefore considered the most viable model for modern politics. Consequently, multi-party politics will usher in a democratic political culture in Africa (Chabal, 2009: 3–6).

But Bayart argues that Africa's struggle for democracy ended as soon as it started. Since 1989, political change on the continent has neither been part of a "democratic transition," nor a "transition to a market economy." He further argues that power relations of that time "did not work to the advantage of the proponents of democracy, partly through their own fault" (Bayart, 2009: xxiii). Was it history, culture or the economies, or all three, that subverted those power relations? Shaffer's (2000) study of democracy in Senegal reveals African democracy can only be effective when it is embedded within African cultural and social thoughts. For Senegalese, collective security rather than elections is the primary goal of democracy. This is clearly demonstrated in the kinds of rhetoric that have emerged to contest President Sall's legitimacy. The existing forms of social mobilization are another indication that Senegalese are redefining their democracy based on Senegalese terms. Political progress has to match the social and cultural visions of its specific context. Therefore, political success should be measured using African cultural logics and moral matrixes (see Schatzberg, 2001).

The rhetorical power JITs dispense indicate that democracy has to be founded on truth, justice and morality. Schatzberg argues that morality has been a deep-rooted political concern in most premodern African states. There is no doubt that African politics is as complex as that of any other region of the world. However, using African perspectives to analyze African politics can have rewarding returns for understanding the true nature of politics on the continent. The "politics of the belly," which Bayart identifies as part of the patrimonial bearing of African politics, can best be understood as a legacy of the colonial state that was reinvented in the postcolonial era. The demands of JIT movements can also be understood as appeals for embedding the African state within an organic African frame.

In both The Gambia and Guinea-Bissau, the growing popularity of indigenous philosophical conceptions of statehood and the functioning of the state are becoming a central part of the discourses about democracy and statehood. This also applies in Senegal and Mali (see Chapter 3). Issues like state–society relations, the status of power and authority or how the state extends into society have long been issues of concern to Africanist scholarship. Initial studies of the African state explored the formal structures and the roles state institutions serve in governance. Society's day-to-day experiences of the state were isolated from such studies (Harsch, 1997). History was largely studied in relation to the postcolonial African state's colonial past. But it did not focus on the importance historical knowledge has for solid statehood.

Harris argues that historical knowledge gives the individual or society a sense of self and being. It creates a durable path that helps the individual to put in perspective relationships with the self, others, nature and with "some superior idea of Being" (Harris, 2003: 113). It coordinates thought and action, helps individuals find their worth within a secure communal fold that can accurately project and appreciate reality through a "collective and nurturing tradition" humanity can attach itself to (Harris, 2003: 115). Barry thinks the unhelpful relationship the postcolonial African state has toward history impacted its logic and functions. He argues: "A reading of our history, recent and remote, shows that ... We do have a history ... The problem is that we still live outside our history. That is because in the abundance of political rhetoric flowing from our states, and in all their activities, serious thinking about the experience of our societies is rare" (Barry 1998: xiii). In the absence of history, culture and the lived realities of society, statehood becomes more of an illusion than a realizable goal.

Scholars like Callaghy (1984, quoted in Harsch, 1997) brought history into the study of the African state by comparing them with early European states. They connect them with Weberian patrimonial governance structures. While this approach connected the state to society, it does not give it a prominent role in shaping viable statehood. Rothchild and Chazan (1988) use a state/civil society complex to draw the connections between the state (represented as autonomous) and society. In this model, society is antagonistic to the state as the two operate on different logics. The state–society complex emphasizes individual over communal rights. Civil society is generally suspicious of the state's relation to human rights; the state in turn mistrusts civil society's instrumentalization of human rights, which it considers a tool for political chaos. This state–civil society approach therefore rests on conflictual relations, that pit state against society or society against state. Rothchild and Chazan's theory is an influential perspective on state–society relations in Africa. However, it does not adequately explain the function historical knowledge plays in state–society relations. Migdal (1988) blends the state into society to show how different networks in society connect the state to people. Similarly, for Bayart (2009), the state and society are not distinct entities. Social forces penetrate the state to glean benefits from it. Therefore, society is complicit in state corruption and mismanagement. Thus, the primary concern for the African state and society is power and wealth. But this view does not adequately answer the question what do individuals seek to obtain as citizens of the African state, beyond the material objects of wealth and power?

Mamdani (1998) constructively theorizes how colonial rule has created a bifurcated state in Africa. Consequently, the postcolonial state that inherited the legacies of the colonial state is embedded in different forms of inequalities that cause citizens to struggle to have effective citizenship. The dual administrative and power regimes inherited by postcolonial states affect both the politics and political economy of the state. This means there is a need to reorder the postcolonial African state to avoid the continuation of the situation in which "democracy will remain not only superficial but also explosive" (Mamdani, 2018: 289). These different theories of the African state highlight how understandings about the African state have progressed, yet much remains to be studied and understood about some of its fundamental realities. Therefore, this book fills an important gap in our understanding of the African state.

Viewing the state from below

To understand the state in Africa, one must first understand what Africans think of the state and what visions the state embodies in their perspectives. One area in which citizens actively communicate their political visions, ideas of the state, values for leadership and followership, is through various art forms. They include songs, poetry and various other artistic compositions. For example, in 1956 Gambian youth and their older political mentors developed *asiko* music as a mobilizing force to end British rule in the country (see Chapter 2). This use of music to pursue political goals has been part of a longstanding Mande tradition. Music was also a powerful mobilizing force during Guinea-Bissau's liberation struggle against Portuguese rule. Some postcolonial Gambian and Bissau-Guinean music compositions followed established Mande or Kabunka traditional musical forms, which were culturally used to discuss taboo subjects or to disparage social or political immorality. "Popular arts penetrate and are penetrated by political, economic and religious institutions" (Barber, 1987: 1). For example, Jaliba Kuyateh, Gambian master kora player, borrowed from Mande artistic traditions for expressing political dissent through music. He composed a song in Mandinka called "teli saba" (or "teli sabou"), which means in English "three days." The metaphor of three days is a powerful cautionary metaphor that indicates one must remember there will be an end to whatever one is doing. The song was an indirect political rebuttal of President Jammeh at a time when he was not very open to criticism.

In Mande culture musical compositions and songs were commonly used to eulogize great leadership and chastise corrupt leaders and immorality. They also express social or political views and visions. More recently, Gambian youth musicians like ST Brikama Boyo, the Brikama-born singer, integrate rebellious Mandinka art forms in their Afro-Manding music. His song "Aling domo," which means "eat me," uses witchcraft discourses to express his frustrations with social lies and infights. In his 2021 collaboration with Senegalese artist Baaba Maal, in the song "My People," ST's status as an important political voice is reinforced. The lyrics of the song include the lines: "when they all hate, I love my people, when the rain comes umbrella for my people, stay loyal to your people, don't lie to the people, speak the truth to your people." The song has strong political undertones and denotes the political feelings of the moment. The lyrics can be read in terms of a leadership critique of the contemporary Gambian political bourgeois class (see Chapter 3). Fatou Balanta, a female traditional singer in Guinea-Bissau, engages in transnational politicking in the song she composed for Ansumana Mané. She praises the leadership qualities she saw in him. But rebukes the horror of war in Guinea-Bissau. She also denounces the Senegalese government for its indecent political accusations against her. These musical compositions borrow from traditional culture and art forms. They give a good impression of politics from below. They are also good indicators of the political temperament of the moment (see Chapter 3). This is why traditional songs and other musical compositions and oral histories are used in this book to identify political practices and discourses and leadership and followership principles in postcolonial Gambia and Guinea-Bissau.

Thus, politics is framed using local idioms from local art forms and indigenous languages to demonstrate local understandings of politics. For example, a Wollof phrase "Kumba bu am ndey, ak Kumba bu amot ndey" ("the Kumba whose mum is alive versus orphaned Kumba"), is used to depict a bifurcated state system characterized by the unequal treatment of citizens. This political metaphor is derived from a fable that exists in both Wollof and Mandinka culture. It narrates the unequal treatment of two girls. The one whose mother is alive is pampered, whereas the orphan girl who is more vulnerable is maltreated. The metaphor disparages the inequities citizens face in countries like The Gambia and Guinea-Bissau. It is also a discourse about corruption and legitimacy vis-à-vis access to and use of public resources.

The next section briefly explores the colonial history.

The colonial history: in brief

The formal imposition of colonial rule in both The Gambia and Guinea-Bissau happened in the context of the "scramble for Africa." By the time of the 1884–1885 Berlin Conference, African territories were formally divided among European countries. The scramble happened in three stages: first, imperial agents signed treaties of friendship and protection with African rulers. This was followed by the signing of bilateral treaties, which indicated the spheres of interest European countries had in African territories and delimited boundaries. The third stage was the conquest and occupation of European spheres of influence, especially after 1884–1885. This stage involved "pacification," which in contrast to its implied nicety, was a brutal period in which colonial forces used extreme military force to neutralize African protests against the colonial project (Boahen, 1989: 27–36).

By 1910 most of Africa was partitioned as colonial enclaves. The Gambia was ruled by Britain and Guinea-Bissau by Portugal. The colonial incursions into Africa were preceded by the growth of English industrial capitalism, which spread to other European countries and the USA. By the second half of the 19th century, international trade became overly competitive. This saw the beginning of neomercantilism, featuring the erection of trade barriers and restrictions to free trade. This led to the need for colonies to serve as exclusive sources for raw materials of the metropole countries to feed European industries but also as monopolized markets for goods produced in those industries. The colonies were also considered as sites for investing surplus capital from Europe. The imperial states used taxpayers' money to establish colonies in Africa and had to justify their agenda to their citizens in the metropole countries. Thus, the use of race-based colonial rhetoric like the "dark continent" and the "civilizing mission" gained political currency to justify the colonization of African territories and peoples. The metropole countries convinced their populations that Africa needed "deliverance" from Europe. In Chapter 2, I will discuss how colonial discourses and rule established what Mamdani referred to as despotism. This also discusses anti-colonial strategies Gambians and Bissau-Guineans adopted, which included the use of music and song, cultural memory and African thinking to fight colonial domination. The strategies also affected political rhetoric and development discourses at the time.

The next section focusses on the methodology and summarizes the chapters of the book.

Methodology

This book is about statebuilding and politics. It uses a comparative framework to investigate how precolonial Kaabu's latent but influential political practices and discourses shape Gambian and Bissau-Guinean politics. It highlights the evolving nature of political rhetoric in the national politics of the two countries. It identifies some of the latent but highly influential political traditions that have been competing with Western-styled state institutional norms in The Gambia and Guinea Bissau. It uses culture and history to identify the various shades of political culture, leadership and followership philosophies and traditions in postcolonial Gambia and Guinea Bissau. It also uses selected precolonial and colonial political cultures to identify their influence on the modern-day politics of the two states. This work offers unique new ways of understanding statebuilding, and how power and authority are manifested in other areas of African politics. It provides some useful ideas that can be generalized and applied to other African contexts to help us understand better the state in Africa. However, the emphasis is on how national level politics should be understood based on local realities, history and culture. Due to page limitations, it will use selective dates and the leadership of selected leaders to support its arguments.

The book uses oral histories, indigenous songs, existing literature, interviews and newspaper or archival sources to support its assertions. I have used different oral histories, some of which are readily available online, to re-construct Kaabu's history. I have collected some indigenous political songs through research assistants in the Gambia between July to December 2020. I have also conducted interviews with experts and ordinary people in The Gambia and Guinea-Bissau on relevant themes such as ideas of leadership, the nature of politics, views on followership and the influences of Kaabu in postcolonial politics. These interviews were conducted via Zoom, or in writing or recorded. I have also consulted newspapers and archival materials to get more insights into the themes the book explores. As such, this work entailed a significant interpretation of relevant historical materials to provide the foregrounding to events in national history, political practices and discourses, but also ideas of leadership and followership.

A relevant fact of Kaabu's history is that Balaba, the rebellious daughter of a king of Kaabu, became the ancestor of the *nyanchoos*. The work studies what her rebellion symbolized culturally and socially for the Kabunka. Gender is an important concern in this work. Hence, it includes some historical and cultural aspects of gender relations, which were part of the social landscape of Kaabu, the colonial and postcolonial situations of the two countries. Additionally, some of the traditional songs I use have gender aspects to them.

Following this introductory chapter of the book, Chapter 1 explores statecraft in Kaabu. Chapter 2 revisits Mande and Kabunka influences on anti-colonial struggles of both The Gambia and Guinea-Bissau. Chapter 3, which is the final chapter of the book, focuses on postcolonial state consolidation, external influences on the state and how that has affected the vision, concepts and attitudes toward the state, politics, history, culture and tradition. It also looks at the sources of postcolonial political crises in the two countries, the reclaiming of traditional ideas of power, leadership and other values and moral discourses, to make new demands on the state. Popular demands to purify politics moves away from ethnic exclusions, exploitation and the use of political chicanery to get rid of rivals. Chapter 3 is also the final chapter and conclusion of the book. It pulls together the main arguments made in the previous chapters, using additional evidence to support the book's conclusions.

Conclusion

What I have discussed so far can be understood in two ways. In The Gambia and Guinea-Bissau, people are increasingly demanding good leadership, and moral and ethical politics from their leaders. This is also true for Senegal and Mali. This demand for civic leadership means a focus on anti-corruption and anti-patrimonial politics, changing systems of power to redetermine a country's social and political direction. The past, like the character of the individual, becomes an important source of legitimacy for the leader. It also indicates how citizens are exerting their agency to ensure that the vision of the state matches the vision of society. Hence, the state should be concerned with addressing the needs of society not those of particular groups alone. It is about eth- nically blind politics. The second way in which we can understand the questions that arise in this introduction is that in the midst of this new focus on the state, leadership and followership, there are also competing demands that denounce leaders who failed to fulfil patrimonial "duties" to specific constituencies. This second aspect adheres to patrimonial and ethnic-inspired political patronage. They seek to reinforce communal- based politics but critique those who fail to deliver on that. However, it is important to know that the demands for ethnic-blind and moral pol- itics is becoming a consuming force that can powerfully redefine how we understand African politics in the near and distant future.

Note

1 Critics like Gambian Writer Samsudeen Sarr denounce the paying of pol- itical surrogates to commit crimes or fabricate stories of crimes in order to dent the character of political opponents. These two practices were used by some diaspora-based Gambian activists in their struggle against Jammeh and in Jammeh-era politics. Such acts still exist under President Barrow.

References

Ayittey, George. 2006. *Indigenous African Institutions*: Boston, MA: Brill.
Barber, Karin.1987. "Popular Arts in Africa." *African Studies Review*, 30(3), 1–78.
Barry, Boubacarr. 1998. *The Kingdom of Waalo, Senegal Before the Conquest*. New York: Africa Diasporic Press.
Bayart, Jean-Francois. 2009. *The State in Africa: The Politics of the Belly*, 2nd edn. Cambridge: Polity Press.
Boahen, A. Adu. 1989. *African Perspectives on Colonialism*. Baltimore, MD: The Johns Hopkins University Press, 27–36.
Callaghy, Thomas M. 1984. *The State–Society Struggle, Zaire in Comparative Perspective*. New York: Columbia University Press.
Chabal, Patrick. 2009. *Africa, The Politics of Suffering and Smiling, World Political Theories*. London & New York: Zed Books.

Chabal, Patrick and Jean-Pascal Daloz. 1999. *Africa Works, Disorder as Political Instrument.* Bloomington: Indiana University Press.

Colvin, Lucie G. 1975. "International Relations in Pre-colonial Senegambia" Présence Africaine, Nouvelle série, 93, «Economie et Urbanisme» / «Economics and Urbanism», 215–230.

De Waal, Alex. 2009. "Vernacular Politics in Africa." https://mronline.org/2009/10/19/vernacular-politics-in-africa/. Retrieved 12 October 2020.

Ekeh, P. Peter. 1975. "Colonialism and the Two Publics in Africa: A Theoretical Statement." *Comparative Studies in Society and History*, 17(1), 91–112.

Ellis, Stephen, and Geerie ter Haar. 1998. "Religion and Politics in Sub-Saharan Africa." *The Journal of Modern African Studies*, 36(2), 175–201.

Englebert, Pierre. 2000. "Pre-colonial Institutions, Post-Colonial States, and Economic Development in Tropical Africa." *Political Research Quarterly*, 53(1), 7–36.

Fouta Tampi. 2021. *Matam...La Colere des jeunes du Fouta qui denoncent la politique de Macky Sall....* Produced by Bambey TV, 21 March. Accessed 24 March 2021

Gambia Political Zone. 2021. *President Barrow Addressed UDP's recent behaviour during meeting with West Coat Alkalos and Chiefs.* Gambia Political Zone. 3 July. Accessed 5 July 2021.

Harris, Norman. 2003. "A Philosophical Basis for an Afrocentric Orientation." In *The Afrocentric Paradigm*, edited by Ama Mazama, pp.111–119. Trenton, NJ: Africa World Press.

Harsch, Ernest. 1997. "Review: African States in Social and Historical Context." *Sociological Forum*, 12(4), 671–679.

Hauser, Gerard A. 2017. "Introduction: Philosophy and Rhetoric – Rethinking their Intersections." *Philosophy & Rhetoric*, 50(4), 371–389.

Khan, Mariama. 2019. *The Gambia–Senegal Border: Issues in Regional Integration, Routledge Borderland Studies.* London & New York: Routledge.

Mamdani, Mahmood. 2018. *Citizen and Subject, Contemporary Africa and the Legacy of Late Colonialism. With a new Preface by the Author.* Princeton, NJ and Oxford: Princeton University Press.

McGee, Darragh. 2019. "Youth, Reinventive Institutions and the Moral Politics of Future-Making in postcolonial Africa." *Sociology*, 53(1), 156–173.

Migdal, Joel. S. 1988. *Strong Societies and Weak States: State–Society Relations and State Capabilities in the Third World.* Princeton, NJ: Princeton University Press.

Olson, Laura R. 2011. "The Essentiality of "Culture" in the Study of Religion and Politics." *Journal for the Scientific Study of Religion*, 50(4), 639–653.

Rothchild, Donald and Naomi Chazan, eds. 1988. *The Precarious Balance: State and Society in Africa.* Boulder, CO: Westview Press.

Sanneh, Lamin. 2016: *Beyond Jihad: The Pacifist Tradition in West African Islam.* Oxford: Oxford University Press.

Sanneh, Lamin O. 1979. *The Jakhanke: The History of an Islamic Clerical People of the Senegambia, African Ethnographic Studies of the 20th Century.* New York: Routledge.

Schatzberg, Michael. 2001. *Political Legitimacy in Middle Africa: Father, Family and Food.* Bloomington: Indiana University Press.

Shaffer, Frederic Charles. 2000. *Democracy in Translation: Understanding Politics in an Unfamiliar Culture (The Wilder House Series in Politics, History and Culture).* Ithaca, NY: Cornell University Press.

Vieira, João Bernardo. 2020. Interview with author, 17 and 19 July.

1 Politics, religion and society in Kaabu

Being a woman is no infirmity

(A Mandinka saying)

To be a Mandinka is to be honorable, to keep promises

(A Mandinka saying)

In Chapter 1, I discuss the kinds of moral reservoirs that frame post-colonial political culture in The Gambia and Guinea-Bissau with other examples drawn from Senegal and Mali. I also discuss the new demands for moral politics and the kinds of historical and cultural constructs that shape these emerging visions of how politics should be. Additionally, I discuss how music is used to express political futures. More importantly, the chapter highlights how Justice, Truth and Integrity movements (JITs) use pre-colonial political practices, rhetoric and cultural viewpoints to highlight modern social debates about the state, politics and visions of the future. This chapter explores statecraft in Kaabu, an important polity that has become a common source of references in Gambian and Bissau-Guinean politics. It reconstructs relevant aspects of Kaabunka political and cultural history to show to what extent, as Bayart and other authors argue, the past shapes the present. The aim here is to explore historical trends and discontinuities in political culture to contextualize how JITs borrow from history and culture to rationalize politics in The Gambia, Guinea-Bissau and, by extension, Senegal and Mali.

Freund (1998: 1) observed that "Africans have been conceptualizing their lives and social relations historically" from ancient times. The production of African historical knowledge by praise singers, diviners or court officials were ideological in nature. Knowledge was necessary for achieving social and political visions. But competence in history

DOI: 10.4324/9781003140009-2

afforded the necessary pathway for understanding society in relation to any ideological concerns and visions it sought to achieve. Thus, the colonial state, like most precolonial African rulers, was obsessed with amassing historical data and materials on Africa and African people. However, the postcolonial rulers had a different relation to both history and culture. Most of them deviated from history and culture, thanks to their subjugation to colonial and neocolonial ideologies that significantly discount African history and traditions. They adopted "African high standards" conceived competitively to show that their "standards of education and administration are as good as those of their former colonizers" (Ekeh, 1975: 101). Their preoccupations leave them with no adequate room to critically engage with the worldviews and visions of their people. It made it easier for thinking about the African state to be sub-contracted to Western social scientists and development experts. Ekeh concludes that the African ruling classes produced by colonial rule are not elites in the true sense of the word. Unlike the traditional aristocrats defeated by the colonizer, members of this new ruling class did not have autonomy in the formation of their values and in their decision-making processes due to external influences (Ekeh, 1975: 94). Rulers of the modern African state largely expended their energies on "catching up" with the West, even if this has proven to be illusive after more than half a century since independence.

JITs seek to redefine African politics and embed it within African history and culture. Their pre-occupations with postcolonial politics derived from self-realizations similar to those of what Ayittey called the "angry generation of Africans" of the mid-1980s. He argued the "internalists" believe external factors including colonialism have decisive influence on African politics and societies. However, internal factors such as "misguided leadership, misgovernance, systemic corruption, capital flight, economic mismanagement, declining investment, collapsed infrastructure, decayed institutions, senseless civil wars, political tyranny, flagrant violations of human rights, and military vandalism" have contributed to the African crisis (Ayittey, 2006: 4). JITs demand politics that prioritize African interests. This view in no way denounces external interests. Instead, it means people (citizens) should matter to the state and they should be first in the affairs of the state. It is with such understanding that, for instance, today many people in The Gambia and Guinea-Bissau make references to Kaabu to express their political or cultural ideals. Peter Karibe Mendy, a Gambian and Bissau-Guinean scholar, noted in an interview that "references to the Kaabu Empire are constantly made as an important historical development ... and the cultural heritages (including the kora and kora music) that emanate from that" (Karibe Mendy, 2020). The "Mandinkanization" of diverse ethnic groups, including the Manjacos/Manjagos who were not under Kaabu's rule, created a significant acculturation in the upper Guinea Coast. "For example, the Manjago word for rice is *oumani*, from *mano*, the Mandinka word for the staple foodcrop" (Karibe Mendy, 2020).

Kaabu existed within a multi-ethnic environment similar to the ethnic landscape in modern Gambia and Guinea-Bissau. Irrespective of this fact, its culture has widely affected different ethnic groups in the region. Its legacy as a dominant political force in the Senegambia region and the upper Guinea Coast is appropriated by people from different ethnic origins. It is in this sense that I use Kabunka political culture under Mama Janky Wally, last Kaabu *mansa* (ruler), to discuss how latent but highly influential Kabunka political discourses and practices today influence politics in The Gambia and Guinea-Bissau.

Janky Wally (the preferred short form of his name used in this work) is the subject of various popular epic songs and oral histories. He ruled in the late precolonial period, shortly before the scramble for and the later partition of Africa. His reign demonstrated some of the changes the Atlantic slave trade engendered in Kaabu's history and politics. Janky Wally decisively influenced Kabunka political culture, social practices and customs as will be seen later in the chapter. It is reasonable to use his 19th-century rule in Kaabu to discuss 21st-century politics in The Gambia and Guinea-Bissau because in modern Gambia and Guinea-Bissau people reclaim, subvert and appropriate ancient Mandinka strategies for Mandinka hegemony as the foundation for their social, political or ethnic visions. The appropriation of Mandinka history and culture in The Gambia and Guinea-Bissau can be understood in terms of a broad Mandinka legacy that started even before they founded the Mali empire. Dr Mark Christian defines legacy as "what has been transmitted by that generation who fought for better life opportunities for the next generations to follow them" (Christian, 2021: 289). Based on this definition, Manding legacy includes what Gambians and Bissau-Guineans appropriate from Kabunka culture, history and politics. But also what Kaabu learnt and appropriated from Manding culture and politics from the Mali empire.

The main question the chapter deals with is: what roles did knowledge, history, and culture play in shaping Kabunka political culture, ethics and morals? The question highlights how Kaabu had used historical and cultural knowledge from its Mande ancestry to develop a state-system that first existed as a vassal entity of the Mali empire but later became an independent kingdom that expanded into an empire. I argue that, unlike the postcolonial African bourgeois class who inherited power from the colonialists, Mande people were successful state-builders because they groomed thinkers, spiritual leaders, occupational groups that fostered merit-based ethical leadership and followership, to achieve Mande visions. As state-builders, certain moral and ethical dispositions guided their political development and advancement. These values include *Telingho* (justice/or being just), *Forooyaa* (possessing an exemplary character), *Mooya* (endowed with social intelligence), *Hakiliyerewa* (consciousness, the source of wisdom and critical thinking) and *Sobeya* (values for hard work and seriousness). Kaabu appropriated Mande political culture, social thoughts, values, and ethics to build a hegemonic state in the upper Guinea Coast.

Before proceeding, I will clarify how certain terms are used in this work. Kabunka (also spelt Kaabunké) is the term used for the people of Kaabu. Mande is also known as Manding, the reference for the original homeland of all Mandinka people, which is also known as the Mali empire. Various groups from the Mande homeland dispersed to other areas of West Africa for state-building, trade and other purposes. The Manding world created a number of successful empires and kingdoms from their original homeland and beyond, including in Kaabu. They had mature political and cultural institutions, some of which survive today. I will interchangeably use Kaabu with Mandinka since it was founded by the ethnic Mandinkas, who adapted their different political, cultural and social institutions to suit their visions for Kaabu. This book uses Manding as the preferred reference for the original homeland of Mandinka people. It is the dominant term used in The Gambia and other parts of the Senegambia region. It will also interchangeably use Mande and Mandinka as the ethnic reference for people of Manding heritage. The term Mandinka or Mandinque is also commonly used in The Gambia, Guinea-Bissau and other parts of the Senegambia region.

This introduction is followed by an exploration of Mandinka and Kabunka origins, and the nature of statecraft in the empire. After that the chapter explores Kaabu's government and state institutions, the roles women and youth played and how gender was related to social conflicts and customs. This is followed by an analysis of the rise of Mama Janky Wally and the genocide that ended Kaabu's independence. The chapter ends with the conclusion.

Kaabu and Mandinka origins

According to Gambian historian, Patience Sonko-Godwin (2003), Mandinkas can be found in different West African countries: The Gambia, Guinea-Bissau, Senegal, Guinea Conakry, Liberia, Sierra

Leone, Mali and Ivory Coast. They are also known by other ethnic names – Malinke, Mandingo, Dioula, Susu, Maninka Mori or Wangara (in Ghana). There are conflicting records about the exact origins of the Mandinka people. Brooks and other scholars believed they originated from areas around the Senegambia, along the northern borders of Futa Jallon. Hunter-gatherer proto-Mandinka speakers moved from the bends of the Senegal and Niger rivers to the green Sahara when the environment became drier. This new location had ample rainfall, numerous water bodies (streams, swamps, shallow lakes, etc.) and abundant grassland. In the future, water would hold metaphorical and symbolic importance in Manding culture, religion and politics.

Mandinka people are believed to have splintered into two groups: one went south to look for greater rainfall and became farmers of millet and sorghum, two important Mandinka staple crops. The other group – hunter-gathers and herders – stayed in the Sahel and the fringes of the Sahara and spoke northern Manding dialects (Brooks, 1989, 28). "As ecological conditions worsened, people living in the area of the Sahara either modified their lifestyles or sought more favorable environments by migrating north, south, or east into the Nile" (Brooks, 1989, 26). Some popular Mandinka oral traditions in the Senegambia region narrate that Mandinkas originated from areas along the *Kulunjunbe Baa* (which is a Mandinka name for the Nile). One oral tradition specifically mentions *Karrtumi*, a reference for Khartoum, the capital of modern Sudan, as the specific place they originated from.

Brooks (1989) highlighted that Mandinkas responded to climate and changing rainfall patterns and ecological conditions in West Africa in one of three major ways. First, they adapted and coped with new local environmental challenges. In this case, they found new economic opportunities out of the changing climatic conditions. Secondly, they migrated to other areas in western Sudan. Sonko-Godwin (2003) relates this was how Mandinka populations arrived in the Senegambia region long before Mali empire was founded. Thirdly, they raided and occu-pied other territories. This was also an important strategy for the dis-persion and settling of Mandinka groups in Kaabu and other parts of the upper Guinea Coast. The last two strategies were important for the future expansion of Manding. They contributed to the three major waves of Mandinka migration (see Knorr and Filho, 2010).

From the Mali empire, Mandinka migrations consisted of first, small groups of agriculturalists in search of land and blacksmiths looking for wood to sustain their smith work. Secondly, Muslim Mandinka traders, popularly known as the *juula* or *julolu*, traded between the

Savannah and the forest regions. Thirdly, Mandinka state-builders, including warriors looking for new sites to broadcast their power and authority, were instrumental in the founding of Kaabu, an imperial province of Mali and later an independent empire. These three broad groups of Mandinka migrants integrated in different communities and locations in West Africa through conquest, assimilation, resistance and co-optation (Knorr and Filho, 2010: 4).

The founding of Kaabu

According to Gambian oral historian Dembo Fatty, after the founding of the Mali empire, *mansa* Sundiata sent emissaries to procure horses in the Senegambia region. However, *bourba* Jollof (king of the Jollof kingdom) captured and killed them. Jollof was located in the northeast of modern-day Senegal. *Bourba* Jollof also ruled over the ancient state of Laff, whose people were known as Waalaff (the people of Laff), the ethnic origin of the Wollof people. When the botched horse procurement mission was reported to Sundiata, he assigned Fakoli Dumbuya, the master warrior of Manding, to avenge the dead of the emissaries. Fakoli was an estranged nephew of Sumanguru Kanteh, the Suso king, who terrorized the Mandinka before Sundiata and his generals came to rescue them. But general Tiramakan Traore insisted that he lead the mission to avenge Manding blood, or he would commit suicide. He undertook the mission, defeated and killed *bourba* Jollof, and proceeded to conquer large parts of the lower Senegambia region. This territory was first called Tiramakan Banku ("Tiramakan country" named after the general). Later, it was renamed Kaabu.

By 1240, Tiramakan Tarawally and his warriors extended the frontiers of the Mali empire as far as Thiaroye in Dakar, in present-day Senegal. At that time, the Gambia area had about 13–14 states among them Nuimi, Baddibu, Saloum, upper and lower Niani, Wuropana, Kiang, Jarra, Wuli, Jimara, Kantora, Foni, Kombo. Later, these formed the new state of colonial Gambia. Sonko-Godwin also noted that the military expedition to the Senegambia area was followed by the migration of the Mandinka from Mali to the Senegambia region. This was around the mid-13th century. Over 75,000 people, including princes, generals, marabouts, slaves, freemen and different artisan groups, left the Mali empire to settle in the Senegambia region (Sonko-Godwin, 2003). According to Green, "by the sixteenth century Kaabu's influence extended over what are now The Gambia, the southern Senegalese region of Casamance and Guinea- Bissau. This was a federation with a fierce warrior aristocracy, the *nyantios*, who shaped Kaabu's strength and secure its power for centuries to come" (Green, 2019, 75–76).

From the 13th century, Kaabu was an imperial province of Mali, but it became an independent state from 1537 to 1867. Green argues that "it may in fact be that the very idea of Kaabu – or the idea of Kaabu as many have been accustomed to think of it – is a colonial projection." He agrees with Giesing and Vydrine (2007: 4 quoted in Green, 2019: 6) that "in the texts of tradition in Mandinka that we have studied in Guinea-Bissau, we have not found a specific term to designate the political entity of Kaabu, which is just known as 'the land of Kaabu'."

In contrast to Green and Giesing and Vydrine's position, I argue that the name Kaabu is an indigenous creation, not a colonial one. Different oral sources corroborated that before Kaabu was widely known by that name, it was called Tiramakan Banku – "the state of Tiramakan," "Tiramakan country," or "the land of Tiramakan." The transition of the original place name to Kaabu can be understood in terms of traditional Mandinka place name rules and patterns. It was customary that when Mandinka settlers arrived at a new place, conquered or settled there, they named it after the person leading the group, as an honor. They could also name it after the original home they left to come to the new place. Alternatively, they gave it a name based on what the area symbolically represented to them shortly after their arrival. The initial place name can later be redefined with the adoption of a new name that is more meaningful, especially one that has symbolic references and logic to it. For example, the name could come from what they thought was the most dominant economic or social activity associated with the land (see Khan, 2019: 8–10).

Basse, a town in the upper River Region of The Gambia, is said to be named after the Mandinka noun "*basu*" which means "mat." The place name signified the spreading of a mat by migrants who needed succor and rest after a long journey. There are also similar explanations for the origin of other traditional Mandinka place names like Kombo, Tunjina, Faraba, Busumbala, Abuko, which was founded by the Manneh clan from Kaabu.

Tiramakan Banku became the initial place of Kaabu in honor of general Tiramakan Traore (also spelt Tarawally). I argue that the switch to Kaabu happened when the state was integrated into the trans-Atlantic slave trade. It became a predatory state and maintained its power through wars, enslavement of enemies and war captives.

Kaabu is etymologically and symbolically connected to the Mandinka word "*kabonh*," which means to "shoot" (in this case weapons), or to "pelt" (in the case of using dark art like spells, magic or incantations).

The linguistic evidence, traditional Mandinka place name patterns, and historical realities of Kaabu support the conclusion that the word was used to signify "the people who shoot," or "shooters." It captured how Kaabu was transformed into a slave-trading warrior nation. Its use of force was captured in oral tradition and the rhetoric that Kaabu fed and survived on guns, gun powder and horses – all accessories of warfare. The renaming was done to capture its predatory spirit, which was further demonstrated in the self-inflicted genocide that ended Kabunka power. Thus, from my analysis the name Kaabu came to replace Tiramakan Banku, to capture the ferocious economy and politics of the state. The next section looks at statecraft in Kaabu.

Statecraft in Kaabu: divination, the *daal* and *jalis*

Statecraft in Kaabu demonstrated reliance on the cultural foundation of Mandinka state-building enterprise and creating necessary discontinuities to respond to the peculiar circumstances within which Kaabu rulers exercised their authority and power. Some of the changes to traditional Mandinka political organization were reflected when Kaabu ceased to be a province of Mali and became an independent state. One oral source narrated that after Tiramakan's conquest, the area was divided into six hierarchical *mansayas* (kingdoms) ruled by either a *mansa* or a *farim*. Pachana (also spelt as Patiana), Sama and Jimara were ruled by aristocrat Mandinka military generals. Kantora, Manna and Toumana, all traditional states in The Gambia, retained their defeated kings or queens, who were co-opted by the new suzerains of Kaabu. In the Mandinka territorial-military organization, the *faama* (*farma*, or *falma*) had the position of governor (Niane 1960: 110 fn 2 quoted in Massing, 1985: 25).

Under this new dispensation, "state-apparatus building" (a term borrowed from de Sardan, 1999) concentrated on entrenching Kabunka hegemony and popularizing their rule among neighboring states. The Mali empire was made up of 12 federated states. At its height, Kaabu's federation achieved 32 states, a marked expansion on Mali's model. In the future, all Kabunka kings, except the 92nd, the last king (Janky Wally), served seven-year terms. Mali trained and mentored future leaders in Niani, which ensured that, from an early stage, future rulers received the necessary education to prepare them for their future task. In Kaabu, the *mansaya* (name of the supreme authority which was *Kaabu man*sa) came from three kingdoms: Kankelefa, Kapbintun and Kansala. The latter was the seat of government. This rotating leadership model ensured that future leaders were also schooled in statecraft to develop the necessary awareness, attitudes and sentiments for leadership. From an early stage, they were taught that their roles as leaders included maintaining the hegemony of the homeland, exercising or demonstrating exceptional talent and neutralizing potential competition from the neighboring Fulani state.

Kaabunka leadership protocols revolved around three main integral Mandinka cultural technologies, namely the shrines and their patrons, who were leaders of divination, the *daal*, which is the expressed visions of leadership, and the *jalis*, who acted as public advocates, watchdogs, and counsels to the kings and royalty. There were four shrines or oracles associated with the founding of Kaabu. They were located in the states of Kankelefa, Kapbintun, Kansala and Sama Kantenten. These shrines and their patrons handled the spiritual aspects of Kabunka politics and society. However, the one at Sama can only tell the future on issues that will happen outside Kaabu. Shrine patrons advised the rulers on political, social and other affairs of the state. More importantly, when there is a leadership vacuum, the shrines are used to identify and confirm the next leader. They also predicted the outcomes a particular leader's leadership will have for Kaabu. State shrines were therefore important arbiters in defining leadership. Through divination, the shrine patrons advised on who was the next appropriate leader for Kaabu. But the individual selected underwent a leadership endurance test to determine their suitability for being Kaabu *mansa*. The three-phased test involved three major royal baths conducted at each of the shrines, supervised by the shrine patrons, the royal *jali* and elders. Passing the first two guaranteed one's ascent to power. If the shrines agreed about the suitability of a selected leader, the person would successfully endure the royal baths, which sanctified him before he was installed as Kaabu *mansa*. However, if he was not the right leader for Kaabu, he died before completing the course. This leadership endurance test was symbolically a test for one's readiness to endure all the sacrifices leadership entailed, represented by the willingness to undertake the first risk of leadership, which might lead to one's demise.

The leadership endurance test was also informed by the thinking that Kaabu's leaders must have spiritual endowments, be well versed in the esoteric sciences and wisdom. This idea of leadership resonates with the observation of Ellis and Haar (1998) that in many pre-colonial African societies rulers were endowed with sacred duties. They were expected to have abilities to cause rain to fall, crops to grow, keep away plague and to maintain the cosmic order of things. Kaabu's leadership endurance test exemplified how religion and politics have historically been connected to concepts of the state and are important avenues for ordering systems of power in society.

The importance of Kaabu's shrines to its political protocols was highlighted in the story of *mansa* Kanchundanla of Kaabu. In the oral accounts Finna Dahaba narrates about his reign, Kanchundanla was obsessed with changing the four *Tamba Janlangs* (oracles of Kaabu) by abrogating the one at Sama. Abolishing a longstanding tradition could be one way of leaving an imprint on a people's history. To achieve this goal, he invited each of the three patrons of the other three oracles to inform them about his plan. While having a feast organized for them, the first patron revealed the food they were eating was cooked by a woman seeing her menses. The woman was invited to determine if the patron was telling the truth and she confirmed under oath that it was true. The second patron revealed the meat cooked for them was dog meat. The owner of the sheep that was slaughtered and cooked in their honor came and under oath confirmed that the young sheep lost its mother. At the time, he had a dog that had puppies. He suckled the sheep from the mother dog's breast. The third patron revealed that *mansa* Kanchundanla was an imposter king. His mother was invited and under oath she confirmed that, following advice from her husband, the late king's spiritual guide, she copulated with a royal slave in order to give the king an heir since he could not have a child. That child became *mansa* Kanchundanla.

The first revelation was a metaphor and a warning for the king to not proceed with his intended project. It resonates with the Wollof proverb "know all, say all, spoil all." In order words, there are things that are better kept secret. The use of the woman is also intended as homage to the kinds of knowledge women have in society. They contributed to Kaabu's greatness, traditions and rituals, and femininity and secrecy built and sustained its power. In our modern-day gender lenses, questioning the woman about her menses can be seen as a grave bias and infringement of her privacy. But the purpose and moral it communicated was different. Women were seen as keepers of secrets that can have powerful impacts on society. The second patron delivered another tacit warning that there were some things in the dark which are better left there. This was an indirect reference about the king's status as an illegitimate child and an imposter king. The third patron brought out the final and greatest upset to the king's true identity. The patrons reminded him that they were custodians of spirituality and political secrets of Kaabu. Indirectly, this was an implicit contest of power between the spiritual leaders and a political leader. The story resonates with the Wollof wise saying that "if a person forgets what brought him/her to power, he/she is easily deposed."

It also raises the question: are there certain constitutive or foundational elements in every society which must not change because changing them may break society apart? In order words is there a certain form of power that must not be re-ordered? Ellis and Haar (1998:178) note that religious ritual plays an important role in postcolonial African politics since "all power is widely believed to have its ultimate origin in the same source, namely the invisible world." The authors also identified how in postcolonial Africa ritual experts and spiritual leaders attain levels of power that may sometimes be beyond those of political leaders. They are vital sources of information and therefore political leaders generally tended to have close relations with such brokers of power in the state. This resonates with recent events in Senegal where religious leaders organized public prayers where they asked God to protect Ousmane Sonko for them. They also formed organizations that are called the "collective to protect Ousmane Sonko." In particular, in Senegal, any leader who antagonized religious leaders risk losing power.

The revelations the patron made can also be seen as a test of Kanchundanla's wisdom. A wise king would take time to understand the lessons of the first two truths. He would understand the need for moderation, the importance of discretion, custom and compromise. The morals include a warning that a dogged pursuit of power can be destructive. It brings to mind the question: who can change what, in any given society? Are there appropriate discontinuities? If yes, in what area and who should be the architect(s) of those changes? Kanchundanla's rebellion against one of the key essences of Kaabu, the oracles, can be interpreted using the Mandinka cultural concept of *dannatambu,* extremism or dictatorial tendencies meant to aggrandize a person's image. It can also mean the overturning of the threshold of justice and reason. Kanchundanla's *dannatambu* would set Kaabu on the path of decline. Janky Wally and the members of his royal entourage would eventually take the *dannatambu* to new levels, when they adopted *tajiriya* (legitimizing political excesses or tyranny) as a political practice, which finally crashed Kaabu's long-held power and authority in the upper Guinea Coast.

The revelation and the words of the shrine patrons reminds how in Kaabu, like in Manding, the word had special significance. The concept about Mandinka greatness has been central to Mandinka social and cultural philosophies communicated through epic songs, dirges and proverbs like "*Mandinkaya mu forooyaa leti, Forooya mu kanyoleti*" ("Being Mandinka is noble. Being noble is keeping promises"). This saying is the conceptual background for ideas of *karafoo* (entrustment) in Mandinka cultural and social life, which is reflected in the saying:

"*Karafoo ye jotentung saabang*" ("entrustment precedes cowardice"). "This idiomatic expression asserts the importance of trust in the articulation of society." It implies "even the one who runs away when in danger should be brave if the person entrusted to him gets in trouble" (Bellagamba, 2004: 383).

Based on these cultural tropes, in Kaabu, like in Manding, character and the word (keeping promises) were two important values. "The Mande are very deliberate in their social lives. They are taught to value attentiveness and circumspection, to strive for an ideal disposition in which listening and thinking take precedence over speaking and acting" (McNaughton,1988: 64). Through various forms of social grooming like initiations and different forms of apprenticeship training, the young Kabunka was socialized to value his/her word, keep promises, respect elders and to shun interpersonal conflicts with close associates. But this did not mean that it was a conflict-free society.

One of the major acts of a king before his enthronement was to undertake the *daal*, a pledge and an expression of allegiance to Kaabu and what the people should expect during his reign. The *daal* ritual entrenched the legitimacy of Kabunka rulers. Every new king undertook the pledge and all the promises made must be achieved before the end of his reign. Following a successful completion of the leadership endurance test, the *daal* marked the formalization of the social contract between the *mansa* and the people of Kaabu. This stage of the leadership installation process was also overseen by elders who were also mandated to produce the royal chair, hat, dress and pants for the new king. Traditionally, before a *mansa* was confirmed, the kingmakers brought a royal chair and the royal staff before the new king. The *mansa* was made to wear the royal dress and pants. The *jali* held the royal hat to place on the *mansa*'s head, walked the king to the royal chair and asked him to sit on the royal hearth. In the presence of all Kaabu, the mansa delivered the *daal*, the royal oath and pledge each king made on what he would deliver for Kaabu, what would happen during his reign, and this could also include the legacy he expected to leave behind. The *daal* was therefore a reliable measurement of what Kabunkas should expect from any new king. It was also seen as a statement of truth since traditionally the *daal* each king made came to pass as he predicted. It was therefore both an institution and a practice that reinforced the importance of words in Manding society, where being a person of authority was similar to being an elderly person. Society expected nothing but the truth from elders and leaders. To retain social respect, they dared not lie to people or society. Truth-telling and *Tilingho* (justice) were seen as two fundamental aspects of character and decency and were key values for running an orderly stable society. Vansina identified that in Mande lands there is a correlation between truth and rank. The "higher the rank of the speaker the truer what he says, even if he speaks about the past," (Vansina, 1985: 130). Rank, truth-telling and costume are also correlated in Mandinka culture. *Jalis* were traditionally well-dressed even in the presence of royalty to further reinforce their status as people who were credible and who would not sell their credibility for patronage gifts since they had a variety of patrons in society. Dressing well was also seen as benefitting for them as bards, negotiators, mediators or transmitters of knowledge. Ostentatious clothing was therefore a tool for ensuring that the *jali* developed no complex in telling the truth in the presence of other people, irrespective of their social status. It entrenched the respect people had for them and fitted how dress has symbolic values in politics and truth-telling in Mandinka culture. Truth-telling was important in many other traditional African societies. For example, "For the Kuba, truth is guaranteed by the state councils. When chiefly tradition is to be related, the council rehearses first in secret, *the kuum*, to establish once again what the truth is" (Vansina, 1985: 130).

Truth-telling involves expressing facts, stating things as they are, but also managing that process in a way that protects the social good. It can also entail passing judgments without any fear or favor, being sincere in communications and interactions with other people. Truth-telling was both a social and political imperative for the existence of fairness and justice in traditional Mandinka society. The standards for truth-telling did not mean that there could never have been people who did not stretch or hide the truth based on political expediency or other reasons. So, Mandinka society established mechanisms for identifying truth-tellers in situations where truth is not forthcoming. This was done through the practice of divination, which could identify truth-tellers, concealed facts and other non-obvious human behavior, or things about the past, present or the future. Divination has been an important practice in various African cultures. For example, "Diviners are common in Rundi oral traditions and their predictions about the future always comes true" (Vansina, 1985: 132). Oath-taking was also an important mechanism for establishing truth. More recently, in both Gambian and Senegalese politics, people have now integrated oath-taking as informal political practices where opponents who they believed are being uncooperative with the truth are asked to take an oath in public. However, this growing practice implicitly shows the levels of distrust people have for modern judicial processes in society. In other words, these ancient practices of establishing truth are resorted to partly because some people do not trust that the courts of the state are impartial enough to render justice.

The third important aspect for the installation of a Kaabu *mansa* included the participation of the *jali*. *Jalis* were revered for their perceived and demonstrated neutrality, their command of general and specialized knowledge and skills, powers of oratory and sincerity, among other virtues. Political leaders were therefore beholden to them. The *jali* belong to a lower caste in Mandinka social hierarchy. But they were leaders in society and were termed virtuous. The power of a *jali* rested on his demonstrated neutrality but also his character. This resonates with the observation that in some African societies "leadership depends heavily on a man's character, his hunting prowess, and especially his ability to focus people's opinions" (Ayitteh, 2006: 115). These attributes of leadership were also valued in Mandinka society as we will later see in this chapter.

The Mandinkas created and entrenched the *jali* social group, associated with the mastery of the "word" and as part of the institutional system that perpetuated ideas of Mandinka greatness and nobility. The *jalis* propagated myths and philosophies about Mandinka origins and worldviews. Olupona defines myth as "narratives that are regarded by a people as sacred, describe a portion of the worldview of that people, and provide significant insight into the people's rationale for their customs, traditions, beliefs and practices" (Olupona, 2014: 6). Specifically, the *jalis* played both direct and indirect active roles in public affairs. They extolled their civil heroes to surpass the deeds of their predecessors. The epic narratives they produced and reproduced were both entertainments and artistic contributions that developed a Mandinka high art form connected to corridors of power, royal courts and the lower echelons of the social hierarchy. By instilling a strong competitive zeal in themselves, Mandinkas cultivated high social, political and cultural ideals for themselves and created a sense of Mandinka pride, which to this day remains central to Manding identity and historical discourses (see Brooks, 1989: Massing, 1985; McKissack and McKissack, 1994).

In Kaabu, each king had a *jali/griot/bard* of the court, who was normally the first person who communicated Kaabu's desire to consider him as *mansa*. From that initial contact, he played other and multiple lifelong functions in the kingship. He attended the royal baths, presided over the installation and led the king to the royal hearth on the first day he sat on his royal stool. He was also responsible for the royal costume. The *jali* was a public relations officer and, a public watchdog who questioned the *mansa* on things he did and their relevance to Kaabu. He was therefore a spokesperson for both the *mansa* and the population. He was a chief adviser to the king, the chief of protocol to the state, public interrogator of the king's actions and director and disseminator of public information. He was also the first point of contact for emissaries and people who visited the king's court. These duties were exercised with the highest level of ethics and moral standards.

In the next section, I explore other institutions that were relevant to statecraft in Kaabu.

Government and state institutions in Kaabu

Colvin (1975) confirms that Kaabu, like other Senegambian states, had clearly defined territories. They were sovereign. Their international politics was shaped by a view that war and the affairs of the state should be conducted for the benefit of the nation as a whole. Like in the 12 states of Mali, each of the 32 states of Kaabu had their own governors. *Nyanchoo* provinces had *mansas* who were subject to Kaabu *mansa*'s authority, as supreme king. Each of the 32 states also provided representatives to participate in federal matters or assignments.

Similar to Mali, where the *mansa*'s court consisted of the administrative apparatus of the federation, the royal hearth of Kaabu in Kansala was the permanent seat of the Kaabu *mansa*. In Mali, citizens could bring grievances before the king. In Kaabu, the *jali* brought citizens' concerns to the *mansa*. Kaabu had a council of elders who advised the king on traditions and other issues in the state. There was also a prime minister. Under Janky Wally, Efamara Mané was one of the people to serve in that position. It also had a chief of the military. Under Janky Wally, Nfally Sonko and his brother Nyaling Sonko both served in that position.

Kaabu's royal court consisted of the *mansa*'s private quarters, which was called *Munyineh*. It was a restricted area. Only the king, his wife, *jali*, the *mansa*'s entertainer, known as the *kuntinkosilar*, could access it. Other people had to receive permission to access the place. All official business was conducted in the king's official quarter in Kansala, the state house. It also consisted of public quarters like the Sapu Dula, the place of oaths, where warriors converged before going to war, to make war pledges and to engage in festivities. Taxes were known as *kabangho* and were paid in cows.

In both Kaabu and Mali, the operation of peace-time governance was different from war-time leadership. During war, a state of emergency was declared and certain officials were delegated specific responsibilities for the smooth operation of the affairs of the state. Usually, those individuals belonged to the aristocracy or had special skills that were needed during that period. Oral historian Dembo Fatty narrated that when Manding was at war, a *jawaroo* (title for a transitional leader) was appointed to preside over the state. The king went to the war front. As war-time interim leader, the *jawaroo* ruled by decrees and could suspend certain rights in society. When the war was over, he retired and the king took over his leadership. There was also the *suma*, who belonged to *suma kunda,* the lineage that provided caretaker kings. When a reigning king died during peace time, an interim leader was appointed from this aristocratic clan to rule between the death of a reigning king and the appointment of his successor. These people also retired when the next king was appointed and enthroned. Their roles were similar to those of transitional presidents in our modern democracy. Another category of officials in Manding were called the *mansarings*, who came from the *mansaring suu* lineage. They comprised the lesser princes, whose role was to engage in affairs of state as assigned. They did not normally become full kings. Generally, like the *korings* in Kaabu, they had some maternal links to the royal family. Settlements established by this Mandinka model of governance exist in both The Gambia and Guinea-Bissau. For example, in Brikama, a traditional Mandinka settlement in the West Coast region of The Gambia, chiefs of the region normally come from the Bojang lineage who constitute a royal house. The traditional settlement consists of *suma kunda, sanneh kunda*, and *mansaring suu*. They function in relation to the roles the different groups played in traditional Mandinka royal courts and governance arrangements. Consultations and rituals established criteria for access and participation in governance like in both Mali and Kaabu.

In Kaabu, *korings* represented the warrior class, whose services were in great demand in the empire. Under normal circumstances, and like the warriors of Manding, they could become governors but not *mansas*. This group was also known as *marrolu*. However, this title is shared with other reputable warriors of the empire, such as members of the Wally clan. The reference derived from *Mari-Batang*, which was used for day-retreats for new kings and also as the pre-war meeting place where warriors converged, made pledges and promises of what they would do in the coming war, and socialized before their deployment. The *marros* were a special but mixed group of warriors whose bravery was celebrated in the epic song *cheddo*. In an interview on 19 July 2020, Braima Sanhá, an oral historian and PAIGC member in Guinea-Bissau, narrated that the state of Kaabu also had officials responsible for border patrol. Under Janky Wally, they included his cousin Toura

Sané, Malang Balang Kula, Malang Bula Fema, Yerikunto Sané and Yunka Manju (Sanhá, 2021).

Kaabu was a majority animist state. However, it had a few Muslim states like Manna Jamang. The leaders of this Muslim minority community (the marabouts) were known as *kaabu sula koi ndinghu,* the free-born Muslims of Kaabu. These people were given the status of religious leaders in Islam. They had mastery of Quranic knowledge and the Islamic sciences. However, they were considered outsiders and were excluded from directly participating in governance. They enjoyed freedom of worship as long as they did not encroach on the affairs of the *Kaabu kuyo* (the white kaabu, another name for *nyanchoos*) or the Kaabu *fingyo* (the black Kaabu, another name for the *korings*). These terms were used to identify people considered to belong to Kaabu proper, its animist traditions and culture. The Islamized communities and their leaders did not belong to the royal or aristocratic classes of Kaabu. As such, they largely lived in self-contained states where they established Islamic educational facilities, practiced their religion, and socialized based on principles of their faith and culture. However, they could form friendships and close ties with the royals and aristocrats based on mutual respect. Sometimes, members from these groups could also belong to the same circumcision cohorts. Depending on their status and circumstances, strangers or visitors were given what was considered their appropriate status in the social hierarchy.

The next section explores the status of women and youth in Kaabu.

Women and youth in Kaabu

Freund argued that "Precolonial states were often identified with a ruling house defined in terms of lineage, but they were not nations in the sense of a specific culturally-determined people" (Freund, 1998: 133). However, the roles women played in Kaabu's political history embodied a politics that was embedded in structures of ruling lineages but which along with cultural ideologies created a Kaabunka people that saw itself as a nation with a distinctive cultural standing in the upper Guinea Coast. Kaabu's *nyanchoo* royal house descended from Balaba Sanneh (also spelt Sané), daughter of *mansa* Masali, king of the Kabunka state of Mampatin. According to Jali Madi Kuyateh, a Senegambian Mandinka oral historian, she was a third-generation offspring of Tiramakan Trawally. Balaba protested against an arranged marriage, gave herself to her lover, conceived his child and ran away to live in seclusion in a cave, to avoid a social scandal. For seven years, she was presumed missing and dead until when she was fortuitously discovered by Mamadi, *mansa* Masali's hunter. It was officials traditionally associated with corridors of power, mediation and traditional knowledge forms who were assigned to rescue and bring her back to the royal court. *Mansa* Masali's griot, Jali Bucari Kuyateh, his leather worker (*karankiwoo*) and his smith (*numukee*) used music and strategy to lure, capture and bring Balaba home. Her escape and return both extolled certain Mandinka ideologies and initiated radical changes to the future of Kabunka history and politics.

She lived in seclusion for 40 days in a newly constructed accommodation to gradually reintegrate into society. She requested *kamareh churoo* (a pap cooked with a special herbal plant) as her first meal at the end of the seclusion. She contributed to Mandinka cultural rhetoric when, after her meal, she praised Jali Bucari for attending to her, heading the meticulous rescue operation and for supervising her reintegration. She prayed to the court that "God made griots our beginning, may HE make them our end too." Thus, Balaba contributed to entrenching the status of *jalis* in Kaabu. She was a wise woman who brought lasting changes to Kaabu through measured confrontation. She reaffirmed her people's cultural norms and values before she propagated her own views and visions on society.

Symbolically, Balaba's 40-day retreat was a period of cleansing for her. But it followed important cultural customs and practices. Senegambia's Muslim groups, like the Mandinkas, consider the 40th day after burial a period when the soul fully ascends and reposes in the next world. The time structures widow mourning practices and charity rituals for the dead. Balaba's seclusion signified her rebirth. She further reinforced her homage to Mandinka religious customs and beliefs when, after her meal, she isolated herself for an additional 12 days. This was a symbolic respect to the previously divided but later united 12 clans of Manding: "According to griots' stories, long ago the Mandinka first divided into twelve clan, each with a clan head, or a king ... the clans fought amongst themselves. Then the twelve kings formed a royal council and selected a 'mansa' who would govern them all" (McKissack and McKissack, 1994: 45). Balaba demonstrated that she was not shunning her people's culture and traditions. Her pregnancy and her escape were apparent rebellious endeavors. But both in fact respected Mandinka values for honor and shame. For a long time, giving birth to children out of wedlock was disreputable among Mandinkas. She spared her family the shame by escaping. Additionally, the escape signified her imitation of Jumanding Conteh, the Mandinka matriarch who rebelled against his brother, Madiba Conteh, king of Sankaran in Manding, and whose rebellion was credited for laying the foundation of the Mali empire (to be discussed later in the chapter).

The king's court made a concession that Balaba could copulate with any man of her choice. Her children became fourth-generation descendants of Tiramakan Trawally. They were born out of wedlock. But they formed a new lineage in Kaabu, the *nyanchoos*. Jali Bucari first used *nyanchoo* in praise of Balaba's resolve, admirable courage and independent spirit, after she emerged from her seclusion. Her children came to be associated with two *nyanchoo* clan names Sané (also spelt Sanneh) and Mané (also spelt Manneh).

Braima Sanhá narrated that the Sané and Mané clan names started when a *jali* visited the royal court of two of Balaba's children. He asked for a sheep from the royal house. The king consulted his two sons about the request. One of them said they should *saa-nee*, which means give out the sheep in Mandinka (*saa* means sheep and *nee* means give). The second son objected and said *ma-nee*, which means we will, or I will, not give it away. *Ma* is both a singular and a plural pronoun in Mandinka. *Saa-nee* was modified as Sané (or Sanneh) and was used as the reference to the first son and his lineage. *Ma-nee* became Mané (or Manneh) and was adopted as a second *nyanchoo* clan name for the son that objected and his lineage.

There has been a longstanding traditional Mandinka practice in which people can be given names based on the importance of their actions at certain crucial moments or based on their occupation. This story about the origins of the *nyanchoo* names has cultural validity. It validates *nyanchooya*, the state of being and belonging to the lineage, as an attitude. It signifies a rebellious disposition, a high sense of self-worthiness, and an extreme dogmatic tendency. *Nyanchooya* also signifies unconstrained bravery and the desire to not compromise. It is a culture but also a belief system.

The *nyanchoos* were traditionally animists. They excessively consumed palm wine, a commonly consumed beverage among the non-Islamic communities, which was also poured as libation for ancestors and idols (*jalangs*). The importance of animist beliefs and practices among the *nyanchoos* resonates with the definition that religion is "a cultural construction, an essential of social identity" (Olson, 2011: 640). Their animist beliefs and values gave them a sense of who they were, and how people saw and defined them. Thus, *nyanchooya* was also an identity. The *korings* or *koringhols* were the cousins of the *nyanchoos*. Together, these two royal groups became the dominant political class that would shape the history of Kaabu.

Balaba's rebellion had a redefining influence on Kaabu's politics, culture and society. She gave birth to the *nyanchoo* ruling clan that would dominate the rest of Kabunka politics. The pap she ate at the end of her

40-day seclusion had its own social legacy. Traditional Mandinka and Sarahuli cultures feed their new brides with *kamareh churoo*.

Balaba's rebellion is the source of the Mandinka social and political rhetoric *balangba*, which means (mighty protest or big resistance). Gambians who resisted Yahya Jammeh's rule adopted *balangba* as a rallying rhetoric to unseat him from power. Its cultural synonym *"kanasong"* was a rallying call for people mobilizing to resist Adama Barrow's government in The Gambia (see Chapter 3). *Balangba* is also connected to the Mandinka term *kekendo*, the adopted group name for a predominantly Jola group of students at Senegal's Cheikh Anta Diop University (UCAD). *Kekendo* signifies "brave men" or "good men" or "masters" of whatever it is being used in relation to. Following the rapid tribal turn Senegalese politics has taken under Macky Sall, on 26 March 2021, *Kekendo* and *Ndofling* (a Serer group of students) severely clashed in what many believed was motivated by the call for tribal loyalties following the political wrangling between Sall and his biggest political adversary Ousmane Sonko, who has Jola and Wollof ethnic connections. Sall's wife is Serere, though her mother is Fulani. Shortly before these two student groups clashed there were social media communications from some Serere individuals who called on Serere people to express solidarity with Adji Sarr, also a Serere. Before this, mass gatherings in Casamance rallied and conducted secret and public rituals in support of Sonko, who they believed was being falsely accused of rape by the Sall government (see Introduction).

The use of Mandinka and other ethnic concepts to rally political support highlights the dual political claims that are exerting their influences on Gambian, Bissau-Guinean and even Senegalese politics. In contrast to JITs' demands for good, just and effective leadership, demands for ethnic-based political considerations aggrandize patrimonial politics and reinforce clientelist relations that feed on sectional interests. Chabal defines patrimonializm as a system of asymmetrical relations of reciprocity that legitimizes rulers as long as they fulfill their clients' justifiable demands, which are mostly material. He argues patrimonial relations existed in feudal Europe where subjects were also clients, who were treated based on the nature of the patrimonial link with each subject (Chabal, 2009: 93). Consequently, ethnic politics in Africa arose out of the colonial competition for resources. Due to the competitive character of economic conditions in colonial African, migrants who arrived in urban centers depended on close kin for shelter and linking them to jobs. Competing job-seekers relied on friends and relatives to get access to resources. They relied on real or invented cultural affinities that gave them access to cultural brokers who exploited their influence in the accumulation process to give access to clients. They became patrons as "Capitalist firms and the state deliberately provoked such ethnic identification, linked if possible to 'traditional authority' back home in the bush, in the interests of effective labour control" (Freund, 1998:134).

Evidence has shown that in countries like The Gambia, Guinea-Bissau and Senegal, motivations for ethnic-based political sentiments sometimes arose not as a result of direct or indirect clientelist connections to the state or power, but instead due to psycho-social views that the grand ethnic history of certain groups has been marginalized in the national narrative. When such feelings coupled with the assumption that the division of the national cake is skewed toward people from a particular ethnic affiliation, this can lead to combative ethnic politicking. The fact that Kekendo, a Jola student group, derive their name from Mandinka cultural concepts, highlights the multicultural identities that most people in countries like The Gambia, Guinea-Bissau and Senegal generally have. Similarly, the indiscriminate appropriation of Kabunka history and culture is another indication of the senselessness of ethnic-based politics in environments where the majority of the people have multi-ethnic heritages. Therefore, ethnicity becomes a rebellious weapon only when some people feel left out or are threatened by emerging or existing political forces.

Like Balaba's rebellion, ethnicity is instrumentalized during adverse political or social conditions, in which individuals feel they are losing control. Both inspire direct and indirect calls for a reimagination of the political or social system to redistribute power. Balaba's rebellion highlights the important status women have in Kaabu and in traditional Mandinka social and political cultures. However, it redefined political power in that "while Mande cultures traditionally inherited through the male line and were patrilineal, in Kaabu inheritance would pass through the woman's line and were matrilineal, allowing the region's original cultures and its women to retain importance" (Green, 2019: 76).

Balaba's story offers us different nuances on how we can understand precolonial gender relations in Kaabu. The concession on her mating partners implies gender was not a great barrier to people's freedoms. Though, it can be understood in relation to her status as a royal woman. However, gender was not a major obstacle to an individual when compared to age, lineage and caste. Freund stated that precolonial societies had problematic gender relations. But this was not so in all precolonial African societies. However, like all human societies, Kaabu had its own forms of social inequalities similar to what he identified among "Igbo communities" who had their own forms of social oppression and inequality. "Title societies functioned as agencies of the richest and most powerful forces and as such contained an incipient form of class rule" (Freund, 1998: 31).

In traditional Mandinka society, older family members arrange marriages for their younger wards with their best interests at heart. Seen through today's gender lens, this practice is tantamount to forced marriage and thus a violation of both the girl's and the boy's rights. Thinking of it in a way other than that in today's gender logic would seem to many people proof that "socialization into a patriarchal culture entails the internalization of all sorts of values that naturalize the differences between men and women" (Haugaard, 2017: 2). But interrogating the idea highlights its conceptual similarity to online dating, which has become a legitimate and acceptable arrangement for finding a lover, husband or wife in modern society. Part of the irony with modern society is that it sometimes reproduces in new forms past customs, traditions or practices it previously condemned as barbaric malpractices.

In traditional Mandinka or other African cultures, the logic of arranged marriages was to find a reputable, compatible marriage partner for someone's ward. A marriage partner has significant outcomes for someone's family, general life, and for the future of a lineage or clan. Thus, traditionally, before the guardians made any arrangements, divination was conducted, seers consulted and, where necessary, family backgrounds investigated before acceding to formalize the arrangement between the two people. There was also significant background work done to ensure that the marriage would last for posterity and the couple can have a good future together. Such marriages can also be motivated by the desire to foster marriage alliances between deserving families, protecting endogamous knowledge structures, diffuse conflicts and to cement loyalty among families who become in-laws. For example, after the battle of Kansala, Janky Wally's daughter, Kumba Wally, married the king of Futa Jallon. This became the origin of the cross-ethnic allegiance and pact that diminished the age-old rivalry between the Kabunka and the Fulani. This union gave birth to the legendary warrior-leader of the Fulani, Alpha Yahya.

Under normal circumstances, consent was required for arranged marriages. This was established through the guardians of the future husband and wife, who separately discussed the issue with the two people. The elders or guardians also established guardians for the marriage. The guardians acted as marriage counsellors the couple consulted to mediate and resolve any problems in the marriage. Consequently, the majority of the arranged marriages succeeded because of the existence of respected marriage counsellors, who were generally known in society as people of reputed good characters who enjoyed high social confidence. Due to people's deference toward them, they could resolve social and interpersonal disputes. Therefore, a core principle in arranged marriages was that it should be conducted to protect the interests and the futures of the girl, the boy, their future children and lineage.

In modern times, we can compare arranged marriages to the now popular use of marriage counsellors and online dating apps, which use given criteria to match partners and brings them together for potential future relations. However, in online dating and marriage arrangements, the intermediaries are non-family members. In traditional arranged marriages, elders except for the *jali* lend their services to the process for free. However, its modern forms are executed through commercial arrangements. Individuals voluntarily sign up for such services, indicating consent. With the current high rates of divorce in both Gambian and Bissau-Guinean societies, it would be interesting to study how contemporary marriage arrangements compare with traditionally arranged marriages in terms of longevity, marital success and outcomes to general family life. In Chapter 3, I explore the practices of "hidden wives," a recent deceitful matrimonial practice, in which women are called "offices" (the term used to denote the practice). A woman marries an already married man in secret. Their relationship is kept a secret. But in case of any eventuality, the woman and her children will be cut off from any inheritance from the man. This practice emerged as an unintended outcome of the PAIGC's policy that abolished polygamy during the war of independence from 1963 to 1974. It would be interesting to study how that policy arrangement has affected women's status in a cultural environment that traditionally allowed multiple marriages, which was later sanctioned by such governmental policy.

The status women enjoy in traditional Mandinka and Kabunka society is highlighted in Balaba's story. Women were acknowledged as important contributors to society. For example, the *kouroukan fouga* also known as the Manden charter (the constitution of the Mali empire) was codified in 1236. It established women as the managers of society, protected their right to divorce, protected them against sexual harassment and physical abuse, and entrenched their rights to make wealth and own property. These formal legislated protections were informed by women's roles in Manding cosmology, trade practices and in entrenching the cultural and political hegemony of the Mandinka people. For instance, following different waves of displacement and migration, Mandinka traders and smiths settled in new places. They established chapters of power associations, which controlled and expedited trade. They also created educational forums for socializing Mande children and the children of their host communities. These power associations and secret societies such as the Komo, Simo and Poro protected the interests of the community in their new lands. They also had women's associations such as the Bundu and Sande which ensured that the children of Mande smiths, traders and other migrants were enculturated in Mande ways. The women also sought leadership and spiritual protection for their community. Thus, "without exception host societies entrusted their children to Komo, Simo, and Poro lodges and parallel female associations for instruction and induction into membership. In this way, Mande-controlled power associations increasingly came to influence and exercise control over local population" (Brooks, 1989: 35). Women, as we will see later in the chapter, played key roles in general Mandinka society and in Kaabu.

Some oral accounts show the wives of *mansas* played roles that are similar to the roles our modern-day first ladies play. For example, the mother of Kanchundanla was a keeper of an important state secret. Kumba Sambangho, the wife of Janky Wally, was the bearer of the new king's clothes as he redefined the royal dress code on the day he was installed as king. More importantly, there were women who were given the title *musu kandah*. They were revered for their skills, knowledge and authority. Normally, most of them belonged to either the nobility or freeborn group. They were notable for their bulky physiques, imposing presences, modest dress codes and expensive jewelry. They were normally rich, had followers and could challenge men on different issues in society. In Mandinka society, women can achieve *musu kandah* status and become icons of power and authority by virtue of their personal achievements, comportment, physique and imposing presence. Personal achievement was important to male leaders too.

The *musu kandah* had physical similarities to the Nubian queens, queen mothers or female regents called *Kandak*. "Archaeologists have found carved images of them …revealing that they sometimes liked to be depicted overweight." These women ruled Kush from Meroe, as regents, queens or independent rulers from c. 284 BCE–c. 314 CE (Mark, 2018; Jarus, 2017). They were farmers and traders. Some were warriors who, like the Amazon warriors of Benin, led their armies during battles (Sigaud, 2020). Considering the Mandinka's connections to the Nile Valley, it would not be far-fetched to say the *Kandak* is the original source of the Mandinka word *musu kandah*.

Women villains also existed and are noted in Mandinka oral traditions. For example, the wife of Janky Wally's son, Mbam Bintou, coveted the wealth of the Sarahuli in Manda, a neighboring state. Through intrigue and blackmail, she forced her husband to wage a war against the Sarahuli for her to have access to their wealth. As a Lady Macbeth of sorts, she manipulated her husband to embark on a disastrous royal tour against Janky Wally's wishes, telling him if he did not go on the tour, then it meant he was not a legitimate son of the *mansa*. Her husband obliged to prove his legitimacy, leading to a disastrous war.

In Kaabu and other Mandinka states, the youth usually belonged to their inherited social class irrespective of gender and occupational differentiations. The mastery of some skills or other forms of knowledge allowed one to enjoy an elevated social status. The youth participated in warrior groups. They also had a say in society. For example, the youth appointed Kelefa Sané as *dinding mansa* (youth king, or junior king), when his uncle was still ruling as king in recognition of his knowledge and warrior skills.

The next section explores how women and youth contributed to entrenching popular Mandinka values in society.

Gender, conflict, sacrifice and Mandinka social customs

Some of the practices and attitudes that became symbolic of *nyanchooya* were influenced by ideas from early Mandinka encounters. According to a Manding *tarikho* (history) narration posted on YouTube on 12 November 2018, by Sarjo Barrow and Jali Alagie Mbaye, two Gambian oral history collaborators, women laid the foundation on which Manding was built (Barrow and Mbaye, 2018). A woman called Jumanding Conteh, was one of the key architects who founded Manding. She was a sister to Sankaran Madiba Conteh, king of the Mandinka state of Sankaran. The relationship between the king and his sister offers an example of some of the injustices Freund noted were inherent in the systems of precolonial societies, like in all human societies.

Jumanding Conteh was a knowledgeable woman who was disrespected and maltreated by the people of Sankaran. In retaliation, she devised a buffalo alter ego, which rampaged crops, caused widespread destruction and fear in Sankaran. Her brother offered a bounty to anyone who killed the beast. Powerful hunters tried but failed to kill it. Two brothers and youth hunters called Damansa Wulengdin and Damansa Wulengba, decided to try. Out of respect, they consulted Jumanding about their mission. Their psychology worked. Altruistic sentiments overcame her desire for revenge. She offered the brothers the charms that can neutralize the buffalo's power. Since killing the buffalo also meant Jumanding Conteh would die, she made them promise to take care of her ward, Songolon – a deformed maiden who was predicted to be a mother to a future Manding king the whole world would talk about. The brothers sealed their promise and got the king's approval to embark on their project.

In a tortuous graphic encounter, Damansa Wulengdin, the younger sibling, killed the beast. This happened after Damansa Wulengba had already given up fighting the buffalo during their encounter. As the fallen beast expiated its final breath, the younger brother knelt beside it, in adulation, praised her mettle, thanked her for her sacrifice and truthful disclosures. They stripped her of all her jewelry as she had instructed, cut the buffalo's tail to confirm their victory and gave the dead beast a fitting burial. The attitude of the younger brother informs the *nyanchoo* tradition of daring danger and never backing down from life-threatening competition. Impressed, Damansa Wulengba broke into songs of praise for his younger brother, making reference to their genealogy. This celebratory act marked the beginning of the *jali* tradition in Mandinka society. Bashful, Damansa Wulengdin implored his brother to stop the songs of praise for he lacked a fitting compensation to give him. Later, he obliged his brother to marry Songolon, whose hand they requested from Mandiba Conteh as part of their compensation. The importance of this act can be referenced to article 18 of the Manden charter, which stated that "vanity is the sign of weakness and humility the sign of greatness." However, Damansa Wulengba failed to consummate the marriage after several attempts, with Songolon resisting him each time. He suggested they should abandon her on their return journey since she was a mysterious person. However, Damansa Wulengdin responded that they dare not for "when the noble man spits, he does not swallow it again." This statement became an important cultural template for the inviolability of promises and the importance of words a person utters in traditional Manding society. It was codified in article 19 of the Manden charter, which stated "Never betray one another. Respect your word of honor." *Kanyho* – which literally means the neck – is used as the metaphor for keeping promises. The use of that human body part references the straight bearing of the human neck. It connects the head to the rest of the body and when it is crooked it affects the entire physique of the person. In Mandinka social philosophy, words must have the straightness of the *kanyho* – they should be dependable. It is associated with *forooyaa* (nobility) which has two different statuses in Mandinka culture. The nobility associated with social status is hereditary and a birth right. The second nobility, which supersedes the first, is based on character and conduct and can be the reserve of all virtuous people irrespective of birth or social status. This second nobility is the basis of reputational power, which is an important form of power in Mandinka cultural and political thought.

Kanyho has a similar cultural import to *pulaaku*. It is part of Fulani people's "rhetoric resources. moral standards, and social codes that guide an individual's conduct toward others and establish crucial social institutions and patterns of behavior through which Fulani express and signal ethnic identity with each other and ethnic separation from others" (Schareika, 2010: 208). Belcher (1998: 47) states that "The essential element in Fulbe traditions is the display of character, the manifest- ation of *pulaako*, the quality of being a Pullo...." Similarly, *kanyho* is an important Mandinka value system that measures good character, truth-telling and keeping promises. In Kaabu, the *daal* is a symbolic re- enactment of principles about *kanyho*, which is seen as the cornerstone of social cohesion, predictability, social trust and justice.

Damansa Wulengdin reminded his brother about that ethic. They finally gave Songolon to Mahan Konateh, the king of the state of Manding. Earlier, a hunter predicted to Konateh that two hunters would bring a hunchback maiden to his court but he must marry her. She would give birth to the son of Manding who would never be for- gotten in the world. Mahan Konateh had two wives, Sasuma Berete and Na Manjai Camara. The latter, known as Sibi Camara, hailed from the state of Sibi. Sasuma was the mother of Dankarang Toumani, the future king and step-brother of Sundiata Keita, son to Songolon Keju from Do in the state of Sankaran, who became his third wife. The rivalries, unbridled competition, show of knowledge, power and authority among these three women, especially between Sasuma Berete and Songolon, would in major ways define and shape the history of Manding.

The story of Jumanding Conteh explores various moral issues in Mandinka society. Sankaran tried to temper injustice with another injustice by recruiting powerful hunters to kill the buffalo; she fought back and became victorious. Her altruism made her the sacrificial lamb that was necessary for the regeneration of Manding. Her sentiment can be compared with the words of Fatoumata Ndiaye of Senegal's Fouta Tampi movement, who declared she was willing to get killed, for Fouta and Senegal, to attain freedom and justice. But unlike her, Jumanding Conteh was true and sincere to her values (see Introduction).

Self-sacrifice became an important value in future traditional Mandinka societies. Thus, *telingho* (justice/or being just) became an important value in future Mandinka interactions and social and eco- nomic processes. Another story of self-sacrifice by a woman or female for the interest of the common and ultimate goal is the annual sacrifice of a girl to *bida*, the snake totem of Manding. This practice became the subject of the Manding epic song *miniyanba*, which remains popular to this day. Concerns with justice, especially relating to women and knowledgeable people, would in the future be protected in the Manden charter. Article 13 stated "Never offend the *Nyaras* (the talented)" whereas article 14 specifically noted "Never offend women, our mothers." These articles, like many others, are associated with the early experiences of Mandinka people and society.

The brothers also demonstrated important Mandinka values in their project. They approached the buffalo using *mooya* (social intelligence) and *hakilo* (also *hakiliyerewa* to mean consciousness and wisdom). They appeased it, roused her familial sentiments, and she agreed to cooperate with them. After the retaliatory havoc she already inflicted on society, Jumanding Conteh's honor and pride did not allow her to continue to live in the community. She preferred death and became the sacrifice for the future prosperity and cohesion of Manding. Her self-sabotage but altruistic service was motivated by the understanding that, for Manding to rise, the buffalo woman must die, the hunchback maiden must be discovered as the birther of the son who will end the chaos and trauma of Manding and catapult it to greatness.

The brothers' struggle with the buffalo succeeded because of *sobeya* (hard work and seriousness). After a difficult fight, the older brother gave up. But the younger one persisted to victory. He demonstrated *hakilo* (wisdom) and *mooya* (social intelligence) by not monopolizing the glory he gained from victory by willing the maiden to his older brother. That act was also a demonstration of *forooya* (exemplary character), which ruptures all shades of selfishness. The buffalo woman's *forooya* was reinforced in self-sabotaging disclosures to the brothers, which reflect practices of honor and fairness in Mandinka society.

Honor and fairness shaped Mandinka war art. It was uncommon for an aggressor to demonstrate to the one being attacked the nature of his arsenal and war-preparatory strategies. Belcher's study of the Bamana and Fulbe epic traditions demonstrates the value of honor in warfare. He observes that Bakari Jan, a Fulbe warrior who rescued Segue from Bilissi "engages in extensive divination, pitting a pair of animals against each other, a motif widespread in Mande and Bamana epic traditions; during the actual fight, he and Bilissi engage in carefully matched activities, trading magic for magic, blow for blow" (Belcher, 1998: 48). This pre-war demonstration and performance was also an important part of Kabunka culture. It is based on a rule that one must employ fair means to subdue an adversary. Fairness in battle was also legislated for in the Manden charter, article 41 of which stated "You can kill the enemy, but not humiliate him." The politics of fabrication and intrigue in colonial and postcolonial African politics were complete deviations from the moral templates that guided rivalries in precolonial society. The use of intrigue to subdue political adversaries has become an almost acceptable norm in the politics of most modern states. Freund observed that the study of most "technologically 'primitive'" Africans, like some hunter-gatherer societies, suggests that "their human qualities, their ideological perspectives and their forms of aesthetic expression such as music and drawing, are in no whit 'inferior' to twentieth-century industrial civilization" (Freund, 1998: 15). Thus, these early Mandinka values amplify the qualities of behavioral standards and social practices that shaped the admirable values documented in the Manden charter. De Sardan's study of corruption in postcolonial African societies revealed that the postcolonial moral economy is syncretic. But "It in no way reflects 'traditional' or pre-colonial culture, even though ancient cultural elements, transformed and recombined, are undeniably amalgamated with numerous elements inherited from the colonial period, as well as others produced during the independence era." The process of state-apparatus building during the 20th century, a process that is far from being achieved, contributes to the production and cultural embeddedness of corruption (de Sardan, 1999: 26). Thus, the "corruption-complex," which defines a number of illicit practices that are technically not corruption "but like corruption are associated with state, parastatal or bureaucratic function, contradict the official ethics of 'public property' and 'public service' create possibilities for illegal enrichment, use and abuse of positions of authority in postcolonial African politics" (de Sardan, 1999: 26–27).

The story about Jumanding Conteh, like that of Balaba, demonstrates the roles women played in shaping moral discourses and values in Mandinka society. Sometimes, reading the social patterns of most African cultures through an external lens may misrepresent the importance of major customs and practices. For example, Ogbomo and Ogbomo (1993) studied gender relations in precolonial Iyede, in Nigeria. They reveal that in Iyede culture women had social, economic and political power over men. Customary arrangements enabled them to engage in long-distance trade, control the surplus in agricultural production, exercise user rights over their husbands' fishing ponds and land. They could stage protests against men or even banish them from the village. They were also represented in the council that serves as the political forum for the land. Abosede George (2011) studied the colonial control of girl hawkers in Lagos, Nigeria, in the 1940s, which was part of colonial child welfare policies. He concluded the policies were misguided attempts that made girl hawkers objects of state surveillance and control. The colonial state sought to develop a new culture of girlhood based on ideas of the modern girl who was to become, through state intervention and tutelage, an obedient moral citizen. This colonial model of childhood derived from ideas of social welfare and modernization and signified racialized views of the innocence, power-lessness, dependency and irrationality of African people. It failed to understand the logics of girl hawking, which, for many Nigerians, was part of the regular training for girls. The trading practice originated from Western Yoruba land from the 18th century. It gave girls inde-pendence to earn their own money, made them streetwise and gave them opportunities to be in full control of their lives. By legislating to stop girl hawking, the colonial state in effect restricted the agency of girls in Lagos. It made an intimate sphere of African lives a site for its policies and programmatic interventions, which rather than free girls and women, demoralized them. It is therefore important to read Mandinka precolonial gender relations in the context of the cultural logics that shaped them and their societies.

The next section explores Janky Wally's leadership and its relevance to modern Gambian and Bissau-Guinean politics.

The rise and fall of Janky Wally

Mama Janky Wally was born in Kapbintun in the Wassa Kunda clan in the region of Pachana. People from the clan maintained their trad-itional authority even in the postcolonial context and are the trad-itional leaders of Kapbintun. Janky Wally's father is given a secondary role in oral traditions, unlike his mother, Kumencho. His future prospects for becoming *mansa* was discovered from an early age. His parents sent him away on a smith apprenticeship. This journey was part of Mandinka cultural appreciation for self-imposed or forced exile, which was considered an experience that built the individual's character, instilled empathy, an important attribute of leadership, and demonstrated the true character of an individual, which could better be appreciated during hardships. They believed how a person conducts him/herself during hardships in the wilderness was a good measure of their potential to be a good leader.

While away, Janky Wally adopted the pseudonym Numunding (little smith) Janbang (a family name) to disguise his royal origins. He returned home after he mastered his smith trade and came of age. He started his smith practice and was well respected for his skills.

Jally Wally was the royal *jali* that visited him to inform him about his nomination for the Kaabu *mansa* position. The former was one of the functionaries who presided over the latter's leadership endurance tests. While on the third royal birth, blood exuded from the shrine, a warning of the blood that would be spilt under Janky Wally's rule.

While on their journey to the installation ground, Jally Wally cut a branch of the Sibikarangho tree and tied it to his left hand, to imply he must unite Kaabu. It also alluded to the harsh political encounters that awaited him. Traditionally, Sibikarangho had multiple purposes in Manding society. It was used for the construction of the roofs of houses, in fencing or as rope. Thus, Janky Wally became inducted into official Kabunka power. The *daal* was the next and final ritual he needed to perform, before Jally Wally, the king-makers and Kaabu, to disclose his political vision and what he would achieve for his people.

Janky Wally's first act was to violate the *mansa* dress code. At his request, his wife Kumba Sambangho brought him a traditional *lappa*, which he wore in place of pants, before sitting on the royal hearth. Stunned, Jally Wally asked him on behalf of the elders and Kaabu why he had done that. He replied that all the 11 *mansas* before him wore pants to the hearth. But no pant-wearing *mansa* would inherit Kaabu's throne after him. The wearing of the *lappa* signified he was the last warrior *mansa* of Kaabu. The *jali*s who were present named him "our mansa who does not wear pants." Janky Wally got up, faced the people, raised his hands up, and declared:

> I hereby place all Kaabu in the palm of my right hand and I place it on my shoulder. If my palm does not break, and my shoulder does not crumble, I will lead well the whole Kaabu - from Batamari to Koseimari, from Manakan to Sankonla Tendinnyoto. But I inform you I shall be Kaabu's *kedifai mansa labangho* [the last warrior king of Kaabu]. At the end of my reign the Fula shall come to collect taxes from Kaabu.

Infuriated Kabunka royalty and aristocrats like the *koring* warlord Nyaling Sonko denounced his prediction. Janky Wally renamed the battle shed of Kansala as Turubang Kansala ("the genocide of Kansala"). He argued that the battle to be held there against any nation would end in genocide. The founding elders of Kaabu derived the initial name from *ankasira*, the root of which is *kanasila* ("do not be afraid") to reassure themselves and future generations how fortified it was. Kansala was also the royal office of the *mansa*. Traditionally, each *mansa* made three pronouncements in their *daal*. Janky Wally gave a fourth, which was that each of the 91 rulers of Kaabu should serve seven-year terms. But he would be in power for 21 years.

Confirmed as the new *mansa*, Janky Wally declared to his officials that to enjoy leadership, one's followers must conduct *tajiriya*, tyrannical political exactions. His first victims were the Fulani, longstanding rivals of Kaabu. He decreed that Kaabu *mansa* could not sleep on his bed in a straight position while the Fulas did the same. The decree became the source of the Mandinka saying "*nyan fula laa*" ("to sleep like the Fula"), which denotes a sleeping position in which people sleep sideways on their beds.

Other major events that happened under his rule signified some continuity with the Mandinka experience from the Mali empire. The 32 envoys he organized from the 32 states went on a horse procurement mission. All but three (some narrations say two) were killed by the Sarahuli. According to oral historian Braima Sanhá, the three were spared so that they could return to Kaabu to explain what befall the rest (also confirmed by Barrow and Mbaye, 2018). The fate of Sundiata Keita's emissaries who were killed by Jollofing *mansa* (*bourba* Jollof) while on their horse procurement mission was repeated through Kaabu's case. Janky Wally's ancestor, general Tiramakan Trawally, was deployed by Sundiata Keita to the Senegambia region to avenge the dead of the Manding emissaries. Mission accomplished, he proceeded to conquer and create settlements that led to the founding of Kaabu.

The warriors deployed by Kaabu to avenge the murder of the emissaries were victorious in their battle against the Sarahuli, some of whom escaped and sought asylum in Futa. The Kabunka warriors captured some Sarahuli elders and young people and took them to Kaabu as prisoners of war. They were made to affirm that their misery as war captives was self-inflicted. The Mandinka proclamation the Sarahuli war captives were asked to repeat to show that the Kabunkas were not responsible for what happened to them was "*tourawutoura asunta ntolelah*" ("whatever adversity we faced here was caused by us"). It became the origin of the informal Sarahuli greeting "*toura suntan majong*," which is the response to '*kortananta* ("how are you?"). The Sarahuli escapees who ran to Timbo sought help from the Fulani based on a pre-existing age-old inter-ethnic alliance. The Fula promised to protect them. Meanwhile, they also plotted to attack and defeat Kaabu.

The Fulani, who were known for their esoteric knowledge and mastery of the Islamic sciences, were also victims of Kaabu. They monitored political developments in the state. They capitalized on the political rivalries of Nfally Sonko, the Kabunka chief of staff who was deposed by Janky Wally and was replaced by his brave young sibling, Nyaling Sonko. The older Sonko was a warrior who would run away from the battlefield in the heat of war. The aggrieved older brother went to Futa to seek help to overthrow his younger brother. They promised to help him. Through their knowledge, the Fulani instigated an internal feud that led the Kabunka to fight and kill each other. It became a chaotic and weakened country.

In 1867, a Fulani force comprising about 35,000 soldiers and a cavalry force of 12,000 men led by Alfa Molo Baldé from the Forria region of Guinea-Bissau attacked Kaabu. These fighters were also supported by the army of Alfa Mo Labe of the Futa Djallon Confederacy who ruled over Labé a province in Guinea-Conakry. Instead of surrendering, Janky Wally blew up the gun powder magazine, which killed almost everyone (Karibe Mendy, 2020). Some Kabunka who escaped during the war fled to the areas along Casamance and The Gambia. Janky Wally's wife and daughter were captured and taken to Futa, where the daughter married into the Fulani royal family and gave birth to Alpha Yahya, the legendary Fulani warrior. He is celebrated in Guinea-Conakry and has a military camp named after him. This marriage started the Kabunka–Fulani truce. However, after Turubang Kansala, Kaabu was annexed into the new and expanding Fula kingdom of Fuladu. Thus, Janky Wally's prophecy came to pass, indicating the power of the word in Mandinka imaginaries and in the destiny of Kaabu.

Conclusion

The reconstruction of the Kabunka state-building enterprise established changes, trends and transformations to Mandinka state structures in both Mali and Kaabu. It demonstrated that change is inevitable. But there is constructive and destructive change or rebellion. The former can lead to advancements in society and social processes. The latter can destroy and rip apart society's core foundations. Differentiating between the two requires wisdom and knowledge. Thus, knowledge-able leadership has to be complemented by knowledgeable followership. Every human society must groom its own core thinkers, visionaries and people with mastery of other sources of knowledge and skills to conceive and achieve the visions of statehood. Whenever morals for justice and truth are compromised, society degenerates. Similarly, when women and youth are excluded from the societal visions, advancement is stalled. The Mandinka conceptualized their futures with future Mandinka generations in mind. They harnessed the skills of lower-caste people, political authorities, spiritual leaders and others to develop, reproduce and revitalize Mandinka identity over the centuries. Since 1235, the pledge *"Manding suma folol anin Manding yere labaghol"* remains an enduring rallying call for mobilizing Mandinka people. However, the concept of *Mandinka faasa* (a concept that can be extrapolated to *Sundiata Faasa*), is now employed as a limiting ethnic tool. But traditionally it was employed as a mobilizing force for different ethnicities, the psychological foundation that produces, reproduces and revitalizes notions of Mandinka greatness and nobility.

It was an important psychotechnology that, thanks to social media, now remains a major but misused political and social rhetoric in The Gambia, Guinea-Bissau and the Senegambia region. Belcher (1998: 54) describes the *faasa* as "the elegiac lament for the great men of the past which recalls their praise names and with them their great deeds." *Mandinkaya faasa* is used in exclusive terms for rousing Mandinka ethnic sensibilities and loyalties for a political course. In contrast, the *jalis* and the smiths who were among its foremost conceptualizers neutralized ethnic opposition to Mandinka hegemony, leadership and cultural expansion. From the services crafts they produced, the knowledge they had about different things including medicine and traditional forms of cure, their reliable characters and identification as just and truthful people, the patterns of speech they adopted and deployed attracted the confidence of non-Mandinka people who they conquered or coopted. They were instruments for making Mandinka rule acceptable to outsiders. Therefore, Mandinka ethnicity was not traditionally employed to exclude other people but rather to bring people together. The blurring of ethnic boundaries was an important strategy for most precolonial African polities. Mamdani noted the Baganda of Uganda used assimilist strategies to increase their numbers from a handful of clans to an expansive ethnic group. "Ethnicity and tribe are animated by two opposing logics. Ethnicity was an open and inclusive category in the premodern period: whether through conquest or contact, ethnic groups expanded overtime" (Mamdani, 2018, xii). Thinkers and strategists who were aware of the cultural foundations of their people were at the forefront of realizing Mandinka visions of statehood, and expanding Mandinka dominance and cultural influence in West Africa. In their visions, they sought to unify and not divide people. But, as shown in the history explored in this chapter, as societies grow and advance to reach their climax, social groups or forces whose actions can crack the foundations of society may emerge. But this can mean a time for a redirection and, in the case of Kaabu and as explored in Chapter 2, the colonial state brought about different transformations to political culture and practice, which also have their enduring legacies in postcolonial Gambia and Guinea-Bissau.

References

Ayittey, George. 2006. *Indigenous African* Institutions. Boston, MA: Brill.
Barrow, Sarjo and Jali Alagie Mbaye. 2018. "History of Manding Empire with Sarjo Barrow". www.youtube.com/watch?v=P2oyOheY4Is&t=29s. Retrieved 27 August 2021.

Belcher, Stephen. 1998. "Heroes at the Borderline: Bamana and Fulbe Traditions in West Africa." *Research in African Literatures*, 29(1), 43–65.

Bellagamba, Alice. 2004. "Entrustment and Its Changing Political Meanings in Fuladu, the Gambia (1880–1994)." *Africa: Journal of the International African Institute*, 74(3), 383–410.

Brooks, George E. 1989. "Ecological Perspectives on Mande Population Movements, Commercial Networks, and Settlement Patterns from the Atlantic Wet Phase (Ca. 5500-2500 BC) to the Present." *History in Africa*, 16, 23–40.

Chabal, Patrick. 2009. *Africa, The Politics of Suffering and Smiling*. London/New York: Zed Books.

Christian, Mark. 2021. *The 20th Century Civil Rights Movement: An Africana Studies Perspective*. Dubuque: Kendall Hunt Publishing Company.

Colvin, Lucie G. 1975. "International Relations in Pre-colonial Senegambia" Présence Africaine, Nouvelle série, 93, «Economie et Urbanisme» / «Economics and Urbanism», 215–230.

de Sardan, J.P. Olivier. 1999. "A moral economy of corruption in Africa?" *The Journal of Modern African Studies*, 37(1), 25–52.

Ekeh, P. Peter. 1975. "Colonialism and the Two Publics in Africa: A Theoretical Statement." *Comparative Studies in Society and History*, 17(1), 91–112.

Ellis, Stephen and Gerrie ter Haar. 1998. "Religion and Politics in Sub-Saharan Africa." *The Journal of Modern African Studies*, 36(2), 175–201.

Freund, Bill. 1998. *The Making of Contemporary Africa: The Development of African Society Since 1800*, 2nd edn. Bloomington, IN: Indiana University Press/Lynne Rienner Pub.

George, Abosede. 2011. "Within Salvation: Girl Hawkers and the Colonial State in Development Era Lagos." *Journal of Social History*, 44(3), 837–859.

Giesing, Cornelia and Valentin Vydrine (eds.). 2007. *Ta: rikh Mandinka de Bijini (Guinée-Bissau)*. Leiden: Brill.

Green, Toby. 2019. "Architects of Knowledge, Builders of Power: Constructing the Kaabu 'Empire,' 16th and 17th Centuries" (article retrieved from academic.edu).

Haugaard, Mark. 2017. "Power and Meaning." *Journal of Political Power*, 10(1), 1–5.

Jarus, Owens. 2017. "Ancient Nubia: A Brief History." 13 February. www.livescience.com/57875-ancient-nubia.html. Accessed multiple times between July 2020 and March 2021.

Karibe Mendy, Peter. 2020. Interview with author, 10 August.

Khan, Mariama. 2019. *The Gambia–Senegal Border, Issues in Regional Integration, Routledge Borderland Studies*. London & New York: Routledge.

Knorr, Jacqueline and Wilson Trajano Filho (eds.). 2010. *The Powerful Presence of the Past, Integration and Conflict along the Upper Guinea Coast*. Leiden, Boston, MA: Brill.

Mamdani, Mahmood. 2018. *Citizen and Subject, Contemporary Africa and the Legacy of Late Colonialism. With a new Preface by the Author*. Princeton, NJ and Oxford: Princeton University Press.

Mark, Joshua J. 2018. "The Kingdom of Kush." 26 February. www.worldhistory. org/Kush/. Accessed multiple times between July 2020 and March 2021.

Massing, Andreas W. 1985. "The Mane, the Decline of Mali, and Mandinka Expansion towards the South Windward Coast." *Cahiers d'études Africaines*, 25(97), 21–55.

McKissack, Patricia and Fredrick McKissack. 1994. *The Royal Kingdoms of Ghana, Mali and Songhai, Life in Medieval Africa*. New York: Henry Holt and Company.

McNaughton, Patrick R. 1988. *The Mande Blacksmiths, Knowledge, Power, and Art in West Africa*. Bloomington and Indianapolis: Indiana University Press.

Ogbomo, Onaiwu Wilson, and Queen Onoriobe Ogbomo. 1993. "Women and Society in Pre-Colonial Iyede." *Anthropos*, 88(4/6), 431–441.

Olupuna, Jacob K. 2014. *African Religions, A Very Short Introduction*. Oxford: Oxford University Press.

Olson, Laura R. 2011. "The Essentiality of "Culture" in the Study of Religion and Politics." *Journal for the Scientific Study of Religion*, 50(4), 639–653.

Sanhá, Braima. 2021. Interview with author, 19 July.

Schareika. Nikolaus. 2010. "Pulaaku in Action: Words at Work in Woodabe Clan Politics." *Ethnology: An International Journal of Cultural and Social Anthropology*, 49(3), 207– 227.

Sigaud, Joy. 2020. "Nubian Queens and Warriors–The Kandakes–Mighty Women of Africa." *Editions Lifestyle, Black History Month and Windrush Magazine*. https://editionbhm.com/2020/06/21/nubian-queens-the-kandakes/. Accessed multiple times between July 2020 and March 2021.

Sonko-Godwin, Patience. 2003. *Ethnic Groups of the Senegambia Region: A Brief History*, 3rd edn. Banjul: Sunrise Publishers Ltd.

Vansina, Jan. 1985. Oral tradition as history. Retrieved from http://ebookcent ral.proquest.con. University of Wisconsin Press.

2   Encountering the colonial state

Development occurs when it is led and implemented by people, communities and governments themselves.

(Holcombe, 2021)

It never ends well if the first thing that should be in a man comes last.

(Wollof saying)

By the time Kaabu collapsed in 1867, Europeans had already marked their presence in the upper Guinea coast and in the Senegambia region as a result of the slave trade, previous voyages of exploration and missionary work. Earlier in 1807, Britain abolished the Atlantic slave trade. Europeans diverted their attention in the region from the trade in humans to a trade in agricultural produce and manufactured goods. In 1884–1885, less than three decades after Kaabu collapsed, European colonizers and the USA met at the Berlin Conference in Germany to negotiate and partition African territories, which formally became colonial possessions of European states. The Gambia became a British colony while Portugal possessed Guinea-Bissau. The memories of Kaabu were still fresh in the minds of local people, who now found themselves as subjects of European powers. Resistance traditions in Kabunka and Mandinka culture became major assets for encountering colonial rule in both The Gambia and Guinea-Bissau. Some Kabunka who escaped *turuban* Kansala (the genocide of Kansala) fled to areas in Casamance and The Gambia, and took residence with other communities, some of which were previously under Kaabu's rule.

In this chapter, I explore how the colonial state in The Gambia and Guinea-Bissau, respectively, used economic and territorial policies to dominate and control the two populations in order to achieve its agenda to produce cash crops and raw materials for their industries and as

DOI: 10.4324/9781003140009-3

markets for finished goods. Both the British and the Portuguese divided their colonial possessions into a colony area and a protectorate or provincial region. The colony areas were the urban centers where land was not abundant to sustain significant agricultural production. The colonial state ensured people stayed in rural areas where agriculture could flourish, and to generate cash crops. This thinking informed what Mamdani called the "native question" (see Mamdani, 2018:18), which refers to how the colonial state controlled and segregated natives by developing systems of direct and indirect rule. These two modes of control had both policy and territorial dimensions. They resulted in a bifurcated state that exported despotism. As such, the chapter also explores how Gambians and Bissau-Guineans responded to colonial domination by using their indigenous resistance traditions, other cultural forms, political ideas and social practices to free themselves from colonial rule. The chapter's main question is how did local people integrate Mandinka cultural forms, in particular oral arts, and forms of local thinking to subvert foreign domination and free themselves from colonial subjugation?

The chapter argues that the anti-colonial struggles against the British in The Gambia and the Portuguese in Guinea-Bissau were successful because the colonized used their cultural resources, African thinking and visions to liberate themselves from colonial control and domination. Anti-colonial agents used songs or other forms of oral arts to protest and mobilize against colonial domination. They relied on indigenous thoughts, discourses, cultures and practices of freedom, self-rule and independence to achieve their goals. They performed their culture to free themselves using traditions of the *jali* or other aspects of their indigenous social hierarchies that sustained their ideas of statecraft and visions of statehood in the precolonial era. Kabunka and Mandinka culture, like other cultures in the upper Guinea coast and the Senegambia region, have long used performance to democratize or redistribute power and influence in society, validate or pass on epistemic knowledge, cultural and traditional values, morals and visions.

Performance means here the use of competence in linguistics, semiotics, cultural and artistic knowledge or skills to channel information, visions or worldviews: "In cultural studies, cultural performance indicates the very interaction between performers and audience that include: prayers, ritual readings and recitations, rites and ceremonies, festivals, and all those things we usually class under religion and ritual rather than with the cultural and artistic" (Hannoum, 2016: 2). Performing the state depends on the political situation, the art forms being used, the audience involved and the setting of the performance. West African countries like The Gambia, Guinea-Bissau, Senegal and

Nigeria have used their oratory culture to perform the state, disengage from it or rebel against it. Therefore, the chapter explores anti-colonial politics from below. Matt Kendall defines "politics from below" to mean "actions that are performed in the public sphere with the intent of addressing an issue that affects a community." However, he notes that "then not all resistance is political. Acts that are 'political' directly challenge perceived asymmetries in the control and distribution of resources in societies" (Kandel, 2015: 636). Since colonial domination was about control and distribution of people and resources, this chapter explores political acts that constitute resistance to foreign domination. The focus is therefore on how people mobilized to fight colonial rule in The Gambia and Guinea-Bissau.

A further argument made in the chapter is that the educational and governance systems of the colonial state subjugated the colonized and forced them to belong to the state using racialized ideological incorporation. This process of incorporation was unequal. It meant using anti-African and European cultural superiority ideologies to dominate African people. Consequently, different people had different levels of belonging to the colonial state. Those educated in colonial education and governmental systems became the invented "elites" or the bourgeois class of the colonial state and they were pitched against the traditional aristocrats who historically had cultural and social legitimacy during the precolonial period (see Introduction).

The social and political arrangements under the colonial state in The Gambia and Guinea-Bissau thwarted African thinking, which was necessary for entrenching colonial domination. As Africans reappropriated or reclaimed their cultural and intellectual resources for ending colonial domination, the colonial state reconstituted its political rhetoric to assuage African discontent. Thus, the colonial state also performed its colonial domination through the use of rhetoric, policy and governmental programming.

The first part of the chapter is the introduction, after which I explore the faces of the colonial state, the impacts of its divide-and-rule policies and anti-colonial resistance strategies. The conclusion follows.

The two faces of the colonial state

The British divided The Gambia into two administrative territories. The colony consisted of Bathurst island (now Banjul), the seat of the colonial government, and Kombo Saint Mary, its outskirts. The rest of the country was the protectorate. By design, the limited educational facilities were located in the colony. Armitage High School was established in the protectorate to educate the sons of chiefs. But there was no active policy to educate Gambians *en masse*. Christian missionaries established most of the educational facilities in the country. It was in 1940 when the colonial government finally established a ministry of education. Colonial officials directly ruled the colony, while their agents ruled the protectorate where the bulk of the agricultural work was conducted. Outside the agricultural season, men from the protectorate flocked to the colony to find jobs as dock workers at Bathurst port or in other menial positions in the colony.

Elspeth Huxley visited the British colonies of The Gambia, Gold Coast, Sierra Leone and Nigeria in 1954. Huxley noted that people were drawn to "seaboard cities" that constituted the colony where European civilization was more visible. In Bathurst and Freetown "homeless people–repatriated slaves-without social anchorage" were common. They feared "the lustier folk of the hinterland. So they affect to despise them, and would sooner than half-starve in the capital than go inland to isolation, hard work and good pay" (Huxley, 1954).

The social environment in the colony depicted colonial social stereo-types. Existing within an environment where the "civilizing mission" was being implemented, people from the colony were regarded as "civilized" and they included "repatriated slaves without social anchorage" on whom the British depended to run the colonial administration in The Gambia. In contrast, people from the protectorate were the "uncivil-ized" natives who were called in Wollof *wa kaw* or *kawkaw* or people from "up." Up was in contrast to "down," which meant the colony or people from there. They recognized the *kawkaw*, the main producers of cash crops that sustained the colonial economy, as hardworking, but shunned them as uncivilized. The rhetoric about location was also about access within the colonial state; who farmed the cash crop for the colonial economy, who got hired as low cadre employees for the colonial government, and the ability to sustain oneself during the different seasons of their Sahelian existence. The *kawkaw* had limited access to Western education, work from the colonial state, access to colonial health care and other public benefits. The *kawkaw* stereotype fueled protectorate peoples' anti-colonial resistance. In contrast, it gave the people of Bathurst, later Banjul, a feeling of exceptionalizm. These stereotypes were carried over in postcolonial Gambia, until after the 1994 coup d'état in the country, when it was largely neutralized, thanks to political developments under Yahya Jammeh. The colonial state created "two forms of power under a single hegemonic authority. Urban people speak the language of civil society and civil rights, rural power of community and culture. Civil power claimed to protect rights, customary power pledged to enforce tradition" (Mamdani, 2018: 18). The colonized were differentiated based on their location, education, occupation and even by ethnicity.

Similarly, in Guinea-Bissau, the Portuguese made Bolama, an island like Bathurst, the colonial capital. Bissau, which is located at the mouth of the Geba river, was the commercial capital. The main urban center for groundnut production was Bafata in the eastern region of the colony. The Portuguese differentiated the Bissau-Guineans into two groups: *assimilados* (assimilated) who were regarded as "civilized." They were generally literate. They lived in urban centers and worked with the colonial administration. The rest of the population (99% of the people) were called the *gentios* (heathens). They were considered to have a "childlike spirit" and an "infantile mentality" and were therefore "uncivilized." They were ruled under *regime do indigenato* (native rule regime), which was a form of Apartheid-like control. Native rule was enforced by colonial officials through appointed local chiefs, and the administrative police called the *cipaios*. The *gentios* were required to possess a *caderneta indigena*, an identification card, and a native pass-book, which contained personal information and family history. The *administradores* (similar to the *chef de circonscription* in French colonies or the district commissioner in British colonies) and the *chefes do posto* or their immediate subordinates could summarily arrest, detain or punish *gentios*. The Portuguese colonial state used weapons like *palmatoria* (a wooden paddle with holes designed to suck in flesh) and the *chicote* (hippo hide whip) to enforce taxation, ensure compliance to forced labor and corrupt demands, such as sexual exploitation of women. Punishments were meted on rural people in the name of maintaining "public order and tranquility" (Karibe Mendy, 2020).

The Portuguese used Cape Verdeans who migrated to Guinea-Bissau due to limited job opportunities, droughts and famine in Cape Verde to run the colonial administration. From 1866, Cape Verde had two high schools and a seminary. Thus, Cape Verdeans had higher literacy levels when compared to Bissau-Guineans. The Portuguese established a few elementary schools in Guinea-Bissau with only one high school constructed in the country in 1958. "Portugal attempted to create a minimally educated class, the members of which were granted the 'privilege' of serving Portugal's interests. They were told to disdain everything African and to revere everything European" (Africa Information Service, 1973: 10). By the time the war of independence started in 1963, 99% of the people in Guinea-Bissau were illiterate. The colony had the lowest literacy rate among all Portuguese African colonies.

Amilcar Cabral's father, Juvenal da Costa Cabral, left Cape Verde and moved to Guinea-Bissau where he was a primary school teacher. His mother, Iva Pinhel Evora, also Cape Verdean, was a trader in Bissau. Born in Guinea-Bissau in 1924, Amilcar Cabral became the leader of the African Party for the Independence of Guinea and Cape Verde (PAIGC), the liberation movement turned political party in Guinea-Bissau that waged a protracted war of independence against the Portuguese (Karibe Mendy, 2020).

Even with the dual administrative system implemented, the Portuguese had a patchy hold on Guinea-Bissau. From 1890 to 1915, people in Guinea-Bissau actively resisted Portuguese colonial rule. "The populations of the Bijago Islands" and "Northern frontier areas" inhabited by staunchly independent Felupe or Diola who lived close to the Senegambia border, defied the colonial authorities until the 1930s (Havik, 2009: 49). The next section looks at how colonial rhetoric evolved using more benign racial terms, but which maintained the darker motives of colonization. It also looks at African peoples' responses to colonial domination.

Politics from above and below under the colonial state

If the "civilizing mission" was the main tree of colonial ideology, it bore several branches as a result of never-ceasing African struggles against colonial domination. The ideology had to be reinvented with various sub-ideological add-ons to soften native rebellion against colonial domination. "When most American and European workers did not know Africa was on the map, there were strikes in The Gambia" (Dunayeskaya, 1962: 3). Gailey (1965 quoted in Khan, unpublished) also noted that Gambians had a "rebellious culture" against colonial rule. Such rebellious culture was exhibited when The Gambia's river crafts seamen went on strike during the troubled times of post-World War 1. They demanded better pay and working conditions from the chamber of commerce, which was largely controlled by colonial interests. Colonial soldiers used their gun butts to break up the strike. The brutal reaction was widely condemned by Gambians, who showed solidarity with the strikers. The government established a commission of enquiry to investigate the strike.

The crafts men's strike to demand justice resonated with the roles crafts people played in traditional Manding society as respected and valued people who enforced bottom-up systems of accountability. The *nyamakalas*, who consisted of various crafts people like blacksmiths, leatherworkers, and *jalis* traditionally held power to account in The

Gambia (see Chapter 1). Concerns for equal and just pay and improved working conditions were channeled through the Gambia Labour Union (GLU), founded in 1929.

The occupational inequalities menial workers, who largely came from the provinces, faced was a contrast to the privileges the Akus enjoyed in the colony and the colonial administration. Mostly from repatriated slave ancestry, they were considered "elitist and personalist" and were covert "overlords" to other ethnic groups in The Gambia (see Mwakigagile, 2010). Akus formed "a distinct political community" as a result of their Western education and closeness to the colonial state. They had prominent positions in education, commerce, government and in colonial religious institutions. Aku leaders in Bathurst historically joined the British and the other European merchants in pursuit of common commercial and political objectives (Hughes and Perfect, 2006:21 quoted in Khan, unpublished). From the 1860s, Akus were influential traders on the River Gambia. When Gambian representatives were nominated to the legislative council around the 1900s, most of them came from Aku background. The Aku Forster family monopolized Gambian representation in the legislative council for some 60 years.

The Akus' influence in commerce, industry and government was a stark contrast to the position of the river crafts people, who belonged to a rural population more than 90% of whom were farmers. Men produced groundnuts, the cash crop. Women farmed rice for subsistence. Both men and women used simple tools. The colonial government promised to mechanize farming through a sponsored "tractor-ploughing by contract" model with mobile threshers and hulling machines. But the program was limited. In spite of that, rice production had doubled in The Gambia by 1962.

The social conditions of the protectorate people were also difficult. The majority of villages did not have a well or portable water. People lived in compounds that consisted of several modest, single-room thatched houses with hard beds, chairs and perhaps a table as furnishing. The compounds were fenced with "woven rush knitting and separated from other compounds by a narrow, dusty alley called a street. There is no electricity, no plumbing, no transport, a single hospital" was available for the whole colony by 1960 (Dunayeskaya, 1962: 13).

People's lives were structured around "the trade season" from December to April, when farmers sold their groundnuts to "farms acting as agents for the statutory Oilseeds Marketing Board" which paid them cut-throat prices that left them struggling for survival during "the remaining months of the year." Thus, they faced "the Hungry Season" from May to November, when there was general food insecurity before harvest time. People took loans from "Syrian and Lebanese middlemen," their permanent creditors in order to survive with their families (Dunayeskaya, 1962: 13).

Limited locations had cooperatives that acted as agents for the Gambia Oilseeds Marketing Board (GOMB). Communities accessed loans through them during the hungry season. Dunayeskaya (1962) observed that the GOMB and the middlemen who worked with it were wealthy. The colonial government remained "the biggest single employer." Its top-heavy bureaucracy ate up 50% of the budget. Truly, the Gambia is an "extravagance," not to Gambians but "to the British, who pay themselves very handsomely for this extravagance" (Dunayeskaya, 1962: 13-16).

Protectorate Gambians lived in such harsh social and economic conditions. Those who left the rural areas to look for menial jobs in the colony did not fare better. Resistance traditions were appropriated by the people as opportunities for such arose. When Edward F. Small, an Aku politician, brought the issue of World War 2 to the Gambian legislature, war was declared on Adolf Hitler. Men from the Mandinka community of Bakau, a garrison town where brave soldiers lived and roamed streets, willingly registered and formed the Bakau regiment, which deployed as Gambians to fight in South East Asia, including Burma. "The Gambian regiments were fierce fighters and they helped the allies who almost lost the war of South East Asia against the Nazi, the Fascist and the Japanese. They helped carry the wounded and the war dead and fearlessly battled in trenches and in dugouts and held fortresses and maintained their guard until the war was won" (Drammeh, 2014). Bakau people had social and cultural connections to Kaabu and Manding. It was a town whose fighters were born in resistance to the colonial state. Bakau people's fighting spirit was reflected in the planning of the community, which spatially had narrow streets that resembled trenches and dugouts built as defense zones. The end of the war led to new perspectives about the colonial state. Africans witnessed Europeans succumb to the horrors of war similar to the way they experienced it. World War 2 broke the myth of European superiority over Africans. They realized that the democracy, liberty and human dignity Europeans propagated during the war did not apply to African subjects who had helped them fight and win the war. Africans armed themselves with the same propaganda to demand their independence from colonial domination and requested more political involvement in the running of the colony.

By 1947, Gambians were elected to the legislative council, which made laws for the colony. The governor, who reported to the colonial secretary, presided over the council. The increased participation in the law-making for the country also led to other milestones. Earlier in 1940, the colonial government established a ministry of education in the colony. Sir John Mahoney, a speaker of the legislative council, became the first Gambian to be knighted. The colonial government appointed four non-elected chiefs who had the same voting rights as the elected members of the legislature. Previously, the (Seyfou) chief of Kombo St Mary's was removed by the British for his anti-colonial stance. But by 1950, the first *mansa bengho* (chiefs conference) was held in Sukuta, a predominantly Mandinka settlement. A second *mansa bengho* was later held in Brikama, another Mandinka settlement.

The shift in colonial policy was designed to assuage anger from protectorate people, who were the severest resisters of the colonial state. In the post-World War 2 milieu, the state toned down the "civilizing mission" rhetoric and gave prominence to "Africanization," a British policy that aimed to employ more Gambians to man the lower cadre of the civil service. But the policy largely benefited the Wollof and the Akus, 50% of whom served in those positions. The "Africanization" policy was therefore structured around ethnic considerations. Some ethnic groups were given additional grounds to get involved in the colonial government, whereas others known to resist the colonial system continued to be excluded.

By 1951, Reverend John Colley Faye (popularly known as J.C. Faye) became the first Gambian to set up a political party, the Democratic Congress Alliance (DCA). Pierre Sarr Njie (or P.S. Njie), an attorney in the colonial courts who represented the colony, founded the United Party (UP). A third party, the Muslim Congress Party (MCP), was set up by Alieu Garba Jahumba. The MCP later merged with Faye's DCA to form the Gambia Democratic Party (GDP). Although these parties were not set up on ethnic lines, all the party heads had Wollof/Serere ethnic affiliations. Faye and Njie were Christians and Jahumpa was a Muslim. It appeared from the outset that colonial politics reflected the ethnic-based privileges associated with the colonial system. In 1958, Dawda Kairaba Jawara, a veterinarian and a Mandinka from rural Gambia, was selected by people from the protectorate to lead the Protectorate People's Party (PPP). It was symbolic that the man who was known for taking care of the livestock of protectorate people was considered a fitting shepherd to led the people in their struggle against colonial domination.

Traditional Mandinka leadership selection protocols led to Jawara's selection as the leader of the PPP. Similar to what happened in Kaabu when Janky Wally was selected *mansa* (see Chapter 1), a group of

Mandinka elders in the protectorate met and deliberated on the best candidates to lead their party. Jawara was invited as the second choice, after the first declined. He was an attractive candidate. He was from the *gkarankeh* (leatherworker) caste, which is part of the *nyamakala*. Traditionally, people of the artisan caste were considered reliable, trustworthy, humble and knowledgeable. They played roles as mediators, witnesses to transactions, healers, service providers, etc. (see Chapter 1). Additionally, Jawara had Western education and was a curer of animals. Herding was culturally considered an occupation that developed good leadership qualities in people. His profession and background secured public confidence in his ability to lead the anti-colonial struggle.

Jawara's socialization made it easy for him to expand the focus of the PPP. Soon it was renamed the People's Progressive Party (PPP) to reflect a more inclusive membership and agenda. Its blue party color was symbolic to represent the River Gambia, a vital resource for The Gambia. Through the river, colonizers came to the country. Through it, tons of groundnuts and other crops were transported from the protectorate to the colony and to Europe. Through it, different goods arrived in the country from overseas. Through it, and thanks to river transport, people traveled from place to place in the country. Through it, people obtained fish to eat and live, and it provided water to many different communities for different purposes. It was an extension of the cosmic importance water had in Mandinka culture and traditions (see Chapter 1). It also represented the sky, the source of rain water, which fed farms and made crops grow.

The party colors adopted in anti-colonial politics bore messages. Some of the current party colors were borrowed from that time. UP was green (the current party color of APRC). PPP retained its blue color. DCA's yellow is now the party color for United Democratic Party (UDP). But the modern party colors do not share the purpose and commitment the anti-colonial party colors represented then.

As party politics began in 1958, "Africanization" was contested by the PPP's "Gambianization" counter-policy. The background and the relations each of the party leaders had with the colonial government influenced their attitude toward the colonial state. PPP was ready for a revolution to immediately end colonial rule. In contrast, P.S. Njie wanted "evolution, not revolution" against the colonial state. His vision was a Gambia that would for long depend on Britain. He agreed to the idea of self-government. But one that would not cut off The Gambia from Britain, because it was not quarrelling with the latter. His campaign slogan in 1962 was "The Gambia is in no hurry" for independence. This position was contested even within his own party. A UP member counter-argued:

You can't manage a country when you are not a citizen of that country. Europeans know their land; we know ours. The British know the United Kingdom; we know The Gambia. A farmer knows how to farm and we know how to manage ourselves. It is time we did so. It is time the British learned we intend to do so.

(unnamed UP Organizer quoted in Dunayeskaya, 1962: 13–16)

Jawara demanded internal self-government in 1961 and independence by 1962. The urgency of PPP's political demands was encapsulated in the prevailing anti-colonial rhetoric, "how we suffer," a phrase that embodied the suffering of people from the protectorate and the colony. The phrase was also a response to "talk, talk, talk, and no action" politics. These two expressions had huge political implications for colonial politics. They fragmented trade union politics. J.R. Foster, the leader of GLU, faced strong opposition by 1960 due to his support for the colonial state. Some members of GLU broke away to form the Gambia Workers Union (GWU), which by 1960 had 9,000 members. Opposing the nationalists' cause was seen as an unforgiveable act of betrayal. The party of J.C. Faye, who opposed youth protesters demanding more rights, better situations and political participation from the colonial administration in 1960, had only one seat in the legislature by 1961. "Taking action" became the desirable slogan. The rhetoric resonated with the Mandinka concept *"bara"* which means work. The word *"baranyhini"* which means "seeker of work" was already a popular term used for seasonal workers (including strange farmers) who frequented The Gambia in search of work. The idea distinguished between the doer and the talker. In Kaabu, one of the important aspects of the *daal* was to prove leaders were doers rather than talkers (see Chapter 1).

The Bathurst bourgeois class represented by J.C. Faye and P.S. Njie were comfortable with the continuation of the colonial relationship between The Gambia and Britain. Their positions were partly influenced by a lack of confidence in The Gambia's ability to stand on its own. This view did not appreciate that various precolonial states had existed and survived in The Gambia for hundreds of years. There was also ignorance about the fact that "The Gambia had always been self-supporting, and in the period of attachment to Sierra Leone in the nineteenth century had been the most prosperous of the two areas. With the exception of only a few years, the revenue of the Colony in the forty-year period after 1900 had consistently exceeded expenditure" (Gailey, 1965: 166 quoted in Khan, unpublished). In contrast, Jawara, who came from a culture with a long and proud history as state-builders in West Africa, was not deterred by the assumption that The Gambia was an "improbable state" and should be merged with Senegal or should continue to depend on Britain. Faye and Njie were part of what Ekeh (1975) called the bourgeois class created by the colonial system and therefore they owed their legitimacy to the system. So, the myth that The Gambia could not be a state was acceptable since it would further entrench their positions.

By 1959, when the "Bread and Butter" strike took place, the legitimacy of Njie and Faye was seriously threatened. Bathurst-based nationalists, nicknamed "the High Park Group" by the colonial government, and the labor movement organized the strike. They demanded better wages and freedom from colonial rule. Alex Lennox-Boyd, the British secretary of state for the colonies, visited The Gambia in 1959. He faced a huge campaign for ending colonial rule. The history and entrenched nature of hunger in colonial Gambia made food an important organizing anti-colonial platform. The strike coincided with the founding of the PPP and both had decisive outcomes in colonial politics as the divisions in colonial society widened.

As the colonial state disbanded the "High Park Group," anti-colonial grassroots mobilization integrated an important Mandinka social and political tradition – the use of oral arts and music to express and demand the fulfilling of societal aspirations. On 2 August 2020, Dr Adama Mbodj, a Gambian educator, recalled that in 1958–1959, PPP supporters founded a new anti-colonial Mandinka musical genre called *asiko*. World War 2 veterans who joined the PPP formed a paramilitary force. They recruited youths between the ages of 20 and 30 into the party. Veteran soldiers drilled the youth wing and formed them into foot soldiers. The PPP Youth Association members marched many miles from village to village accompanied by *asiko*. They entertained and mobilized people and passed on anti-colonial messages. They set up a PPP youth branch in any village or town they performed in.

Asiko is an instrument of political emancipation. Initially, former Gambian colonial soldiers used it as an anti-colonial musical genre and song. It was also a work song for youths hired to offload trucks that carried groundnuts from the rural areas to the port in Bathurst. It was an avenue that recruited district chiefs into the anti-colonial mission of the PPP. Dunayeskaya (1962) witnessed an *asiko* event and described it thus:

> The PPP truck, a minstrel shouting out that "D. K. will speak," a single drumbeat, and in a few minutes under the *bantaba* (a shady tree where villagers gather to discuss) ... The meeting might be preceded or followed by *asico*, the PPP's own musical invention, a

combination of folk and jazz in praise of the leader. A few drums beat out the tune, the leader of the ban speaks it, the solo soprano sings it, and the chorus repeats it.

(Dunayeskaya, 1962: 14)

The late chief Sanjally Bojang, whose family are traditional Mandinka rulers and founders of Brikama, worked as a Steve Dore contractor at Bathurst port. As he was a large-scale contractor, the youth who came to Bathurst registered with him as laborers or dockers for loading the ships of groundnuts. This role gave him additional leverage to recruit and mobilize youth for the PPP's anti-colonial mission. Bojang and other notable Mandinka elders like Njundu Touray, Famara Wassu Janneh and others became chief advisers to Jawara. Mbodj recalled that these were advisers "who never went to school because access to education was limited. They spoke pidgin English." As people from leading families in Manding, these advisers represented a cultural bloc that was attuned with traditional Mandinka principles of good leadership and followership. They employed traditional Mandinka economic practices and social customs to forge cohesive social relations across society. They were civil in their politics irrespective of the strong competition in colonial politics. Mbodj further recalled that "People will criticize government. But no one was insulting someone's mother. Ethnicity was not an issue. It never destroyed the friendships based on traditions and historical links." For example, many of the traders who bought groundnuts from the provinces from the Kombo areas made lasting and solid friendships with the chiefs in whose districts they were buying groundnuts. They were often from different ethnic backgrounds. They knew each other and respected each other. Intermarriage across religions and ethnicities were common. Religion and ethnicity did not percolate in the political battles of the time even though the colonial state did not have equal treatment of, or provide equal opportunities to all Gambians. PPP changed its name to reflect the multicultural friendships and professional relations that prevailed under the cultural environment of the time.

In Guinea-Bissau, proto-nationalist politics created The Liga Guineense (Guinean League) in 1910, as an "assembly of the natives of Guinea." Colonial-invented elites with similar backgrounds to Gambia's Faye and Njie made up the assembly. They were largely native and Cape Verdean Portuguese educated people who were pro-Portuguese colonial rule, though they objected to the brutal methods the Portuguese used to "pacify" the rebellious Pepel people of Bissau. Portugal's "civilizing mission" was retailored as "pacification," which was a rhetorical device to legitimize Portuguese colonial control of Guinea-Bissau. The league leadership were tortured or imprisoned and eventually disbanded in 1915. Guinea-Bissau's incipient nationalism was crushed and silenced in its germinating phase (Karibe Mendy, 2020).

Amilcar Cabral and some colleagues formed the African party for the Independence of Guinea and Cape Verde (PAIGC) in 1956 with the aim to organize workers and peasants. Pacification was not real to them. They sought real change and freedom. Cabral, the secretary general of PAIGC, was a revered political theoretician. He was gifted in translating theories into reality. Even with his admirable leadership qualities, Cabral and his comrades were classified, to borrow Mendy's words, "in the context of the raging cold war 'communist agitators'."

PAIGC's initial strategy was to use protests, strikes or boycotts to force the Portuguese to peacefully grant Guinea-Bissau independence. However, this strategy gave them minimal success. But as the wave of decolonization became unstoppable post-World War 2, clandestine anti-colonial movements like the Movement for the National Independence of Guinea (MING) emerged in Portuguese Guinea. But this movement, co-founded by Amilcar Cabral in 1954, failed due to Cape Verdean/Bissau-Guinean antagonisms. It was replaced by the African Independence Party (PAI), also co-founded by Cabral, in 1956. In 1960, PAI became the PAIGC to reflect an inclusive party, membership and agenda.

Like in The Gambia, 1959 was a politically contentious year in Guinea-Bissau too. Dockers and river transport workers in Bissau embarked on a strike. The Portuguese killed more than 50 strikers and wounded over 100 others. The 1959 Pidgiguiti massacre became a turning point for political mobilization in Guinea-Bissau. It "was a painful lesson for our people, who learned that there was no question of choosing between a peaceful struggle and armed combat" (Cabral, 1979: 16). *"A luta continua"* ("the struggle continues") and "total independence" became the slogans of the armed resistance movement, which had its headquarters in Conakry in 1960 (Karibe Mendy, 2020). For three years, PAIGC mobilized and organized rural people and created a solid political base in the countryside through adult and youth literary. By 1962, "over 2,000 patriots were arrested throughout the country. Several villages were set on fire, ... Dozens of Africans burnt alive or drowned in the rivers and others torture" (Cabral, 1979: 16). But Bissau-Guineans continue their fight for 11 more years until they liberated their country.

PAIGC's education strategy had similarities to traditional Mandinka socialization strategies. Guinea-Bissau was the center of the Kaabu empire. It was conceivable that some value systems associated with Kabunka social and political life were appropriated during the struggle for independence. Amilcar Cabral's vision was to create a "new society" in Guinea-Bissau, one that would eliminate harmful cultural practices, especially those affecting women. PAIGC's political, economic, social and cultural objectives were promoted on an ideology of "unity and struggle." They internalized ideas similar to traditional initiation, where initiates experienced a common or shared socialization and education to develop shared principles to be passed on from generation to generation (see Chapter 1).

Diverse ethnics groups had to be mobilized; the different skillsets required for the success of the struggle were transferred or acquired through teaching, education and training. Cabral successfully neutralized tribal sentiments. Yet he recognized that the Oinca and Balanta, like other ethnic groups, retained their cultural memories, which include memories of inter-ethnic tensions. But it is people who "want to serve only their own political ambition" who would use ethnic differences in negative ways (Cabral, 1979: 62). PAIGC teachings borrowed from notions of traditional morality and sacrifice for a successful liberation war. PAIGC's political logic were similar to Mandinka assimilative practices. They viewed a common culture that was a product of many cultures that shared a "world view and their relations in society." For example, Muslims believed in the *iram* spirits and animist also adopted Muslim and Mandinka belief practices (see Cabral, 1979: 57). This cultural give-and-take was important in shaping inter-ethnic cohesion and social pluralism, which was an important Mandinka value. Like in The Gambia, the Bissau-Guinean war of liberation devised processes of political accountability and political morality that fed from either "local religions" or "customary systems of reciprocal obligation." "Ethnic morality traditional forms of accountability" were used to mobilize people for the liberation war (for more see Chabal 2009: 69).

The use of morality was effective in associating the colonial system with injustices and liberation as a necessary and ultimate goal for returning to justice and freedom. The concept of a "new society" was based on aspirations for "equality, justice, and freedom" for all Bissau-Guineas, irrespective of their ethnic background, age or gender. PAIGC created UDEMU in 1961, which handled women's issues and their involvement in the revolutionary war (Ly, 2014). It was abolished by 1965. But it successfully mainstreamed women's issues in the liberation war, by the end of which Bissau-Guinean women worked to achieve their own liberation from harmful cultural practices. PAIGC abolished polygamy and forced marriages, gave women the right to divorce, and integrated them into the leadership and administrative structures of the party. Women participated in party meetings and were responsible for feeding during the struggle. More importantly, women were taught that they have to protect their own dignity and self-worth.

Cabral identified "a minimum program and a maximum program. The minimum program was to set Guinea-Bissau free and independent to decide its own fate. The maximum program was the development of the country" (Vieira, 2020). Those who fight and achieve the minimum program must groom other people for achieving the maximum program (Vieira, 2020). This view resonates with how the elders who set up the PPP in The Gambia stepped aside and passed on to Jawara the leadership and goal of achieving their anti-colonial aspirations. This idea that initiators of a legacy must step aside, select new people to pursue their ideals was also an influential philosophy among the Mandinka, especially after they defeated the Susu. Kaabu's rotating kingship provided for royals from three different regions to succeed one another. The practice diversified access to political power (see Chapter 1). It invited fresh political outlooks and eroded any possible sense of entitlement that can undermine progress. Inheritors of a legacy are supported and guided to build on the successes achieved by the creators of the legacy. This was another important strategy for continuity and creative transformations in society. Such organized transferring of visions helped to create inter-generational loyalties to social and public goals.

Cabral argued that "elders were the intellectuals of our society, of our genuine, real society. They were the ones who saw things clearly, who understood everything (our strengths and our weaknesses) and they soon shifted" by allowing youngsters to take command of the war (Cabral, 1979: 60). "Unity, Struggle and Progress" became the struggle's national motto. Their effectiveness in highlighting the aspirations of the people is reflected in how these words remain important national phrases in postcolonial Guinea-Bissau (Vieira, 2020). Unity is defined as a means toward a struggle, not an end. It is the essence of their vision. Struggle was defined as "normal condition of all living creatures in the world. All are in struggle, all struggle" (Cabral, 1979: 31). "Return to the source" was a major idea Cabral propagated during the liberation war. It is a metaphor for relying on indigenous cultural forms to wage the war of liberation, bridge the different social and political divides colonial rule inflicted on Bissau-Guinean society, and appropriating the ecological gifts that sustained Bissau-Guinean social, economic and political life since precolonial times. The gifts include the several water bodies that defined the territory today known as Guinea-Bissau.

Some Mandinka cultural forms and ideas were used to highlight some of the principles governing PAIGC's vision and practices in the liberation struggle. For instance, Cabral made reference to Kaabu and Mandinka state-building history when he argued that "the Mandinga in dominating the peoples of our land practised assimilation (the Portuguese were not the first to want to assimilate in our land) and those dominated began to adopt Mandinka names" (Cabral, 1979: 56).

Flora Gomez's 1988 film *Mortu Nega* ("Those who dead refused") captures some compelling Kabunka cultural motives and symbols that were appropriated by people during the liberation war. The film used traditional Mandinka musical and oral art forms such as *kora* music and miming to convey sorrow, hope and defiance. It also invoked Kaabu's bravery culture and traditional work ethics. Scenes show the young combatants and their leaders trekking through deep forests and mud-filled streams and creeks, fatigued but not overwhelmed. The beginning of the film powerfully invokes the indefatigable *nyanchoo* thirst for valor. A boy fighter was given a heavy load of weapons to carry. He stared at the officer and demanded for him to increase his load. The scene showed even young children were troubled by foreign domination and were ready to sacrifice and fight to end Portuguese colonial rule. The title of the film engaged the theme of death, which traditionally shaped *nyanchoo* defiance toward the dead, informed by an attitude that courts dead.

Cabral and the PAIGC party used education to erode cultural alienation, especially among the educated and the privileged through cultural reconversion. Culture was regarded both as a strength and an impediment to the war of liberation. Cabral disapproved of the use of amulets and beliefs about spirits among the fighters and ordinary Bissau-Guineans. He appropriated beliefs about the *iram* spirits to reinforce his messages. However, he vilified them and the use of amulets during the war of liberation. But he did not succeed in making PAIGC fighters abandon the belief in *iram* spirits and amulets. Today, regular people and politicians in Guinea-Bissau all continue to uphold the belief in and use of such spiritual resources. An interesting question would be: did the *irams* and the amulets contribute to the success of the war of liberation? Portugal had all it needed to win the war against Guinea-Bissau. It had better guns, helicopters, and other resources. Bissau-Guinean fighters had to face a hostile terrain that was not conducive to the kind of warfare they were engaged in. They had less sophisticated guns and not as sophisticated war machinery as the Portuguese. Since there is no easy way to measure the roles *irams* and amulets played in the war, one can however acknowledge the level of sophisticated thinking, strategy and wisdom that PAIGC leaders and its fighters invested in the war. Thus, Bissau-Guineans were able to successfully employ guerrilla war tactics in a country that is flat, had little or no mountains, to defeat the Portuguese. The spatial disadvantages they faced during the liberation war was no hindrance to their zeal. By the time Cabral was killed, the fighters were well schooled in the philosophies of the struggle. They felt the pain of his untimely death. But instead of dampening their souls, it reinforced their commitment to fight and win the war. In 1973, they achieved their goal and defeated the Portuguese.

The despotic character of the colonial state in both The Gambia and Guinea-Bissau was well entrenched by the 1950s. The used of words like "Africanization" or "pacification" did not divert the colonial agenda. The terms sugar-coated the colonial vision to assuage Africans. But, overall, they meant little in alleviating the suffering of the colonized. They were largely token policies. The colonized saw that. They continued rebelling against the British in The Gambia and the Portuguese in Guinea-Bissau, forcing each administration to make additional concessions largely through the use of rhetoric and piecemeal developments. Eventually, The Gambia negotiated and achieved its independence in 1965. Through blood and sweat Guinea-Bissau became liberated by 1973. The next section explores how the colonial landscape, political systems and social structures fared at independence.

Building the nation after colonial rule

Gambian writer and poet Tijan M. Sallah's book *Saani Baat* highlights a longstanding Senegambian culture in which songs are used in coded ways to represent events and taboo subjects, for direct or indirect social commentary, public shaming, demanding rights or holding power to account. The British-American anthropologist David P. Gamble also noted the power of songs in Senegambian culture. "A person of high rank is obliged to make gifts to those below him or her, while the '*gewel*' has the right to claim them, and can shame publicly those who fail to show generosity" (Gamble quoted in Sallah, 2021: 27). The Wollof *gewel* is equivalent to the *jali* in Mandinka culture. Both ethnic groups have entrenched bottom-up accountability mechanisms to protect against abuse of power and other undemocratic exactions from leaders and in society (see Chapter 1). The *gewel* and other low caste people can shame political leaders and high-ranking members of society.

Song-making was an important tool for political protest in both colonial and postcolonial Senegambia (see Chapter 3). For instance,

Wollof women had a biting anti-colonial song, the translation of which is produced below:

> I went to Colobane, my hen laid eggs but died
> I returned to Colobane, my hen laid eggs but died
> I began talking, talking, talking to the hen
> Daddy white man told me "leave it with me, I will talk to it"
> But the one who denies you mango leaves will never give you its fruit.

The song is a social commentary. It condemns the colonial state as one that was intent on killing African agency, which is represented by the second personae in the song, who seeks to replace the woman in her hen-talking ritual when in fact he does not understand it. He promises to raise the hen from death to appease her. The colonial system was designed to make the African dependent. It made empty promises, and promised the African meager benefits. The colonial state takes the mango fruits and the trees and would not even let Africans have the leaves, which it had no use for. The song is therefore about the sorrows of the colonized and the pretensions of the colonial state. The lyrics of the Mandinka song below give another dimension of how power is traditionally challenged from below.

> Mba Nyalin, do you know my mother?
> I know your mother. Mansa killed your mother
> Why did he killed her?
> Because she spilled some oil
> Is spilling oil a crime to kill someone for?
> If I am not dead today, Mansa will bring back my mother

This song denounces the irrational use of power and the abuse of women. Mba Nyalin is the authoritative woman the interrogator finds answers from about a missing mother. She has the status of a *musu kandah* and is not afraid to share the truth she knows (see Chapter 1). More importantly, the interrogator is determined to fight the injustice against the mother and would not give up as long as he/she lives. One importance of the song is the need to speak truth to power, question authority but also resist abuses of power. Social ills must be disclosed without fear.

Songs like these two have been used to inform political visions, develop rhetoric and contest power. The *asiko* music was born from such indigenous musical traditions. Politics concerns "very complex human relations that one entertains with others – be it ordinary people or state officials" and implies "the ensemble of strategies and tactics one deploys to manage these relations that are always changing" (Hannoum, 2016: 2), as such music offered the colonized a peaceful but powerful way of resisting injustices of power through expressing and channeling political and social visions.

The use of peaceful resistance strategies continued after 1965 when The Gambia became independent. In politics and administration, Mandinka leadership and followership values influenced Jawara. Symbolically, the house of representatives had 32 seats, which remind of the 32 states of Kaabu. Later, the seats were increased to 35. Bathurst, named after Earl Bathurst, was changed to Banjul in 1973. The new name originated from a Mandinka word *banjullo*, a reference for a locally sourced rope on the island and its vicinities. Symbolically, the name implied Jawara's task to unite The Gambia following the divisions colonial rule created.

Principles of *telingho* (fairness and justice) were the rhetorical mantra of his new administration and were understood to politically mean fair distribution of income and fair distribution of economic activity between Banjul and the provinces. These lofty goals can be evaluated relative to their success or lack of success in achieving the overall vision Jawara developed. However, since the task here is to show how rhetoric and culture were used to express and pursue political visions, I limit myself to how Jawara's initial politics showed influences of Mandinka leadership and followership ethics. The government was brought closer to the people by ending the colonial isolation of some communities. The administrative machinery was extended, additional educational facilities created, roads constructed to improve communication and a radio station was also established. All these helped to bring people together. The nation was conceived as a shared vision that each citizen had responsibilities toward achieving. The idea of a common consciousness was forged under the philosophy of "*tesito*," which is an important farming metaphor and agricultural practice in Mandinka. It denotes both capitalist and socialist notions of work and progress. It became a mobilizing concept for communities to engage in self-help projects where they volunteer personal, monetary or in-kind contributions toward community projects, such as joint communal road improvement works, school, daycare or community well constructions. The community wells were modeled on "*mansa kolons*" (public wells) in Mandinka culture in which such water resources or certain waterbodies were designated for specific uses that community members comply with.

Tesito had a tradition in Mandinka societies (see Khan, 2014: 773). It was a way of fulfilling individual and social needs. It also ensured individual and group accountability.

By 1980, the government noted that "Gambians in all walks of life – farmers, businessmen, carpenters, civil servants and laborers – have responded positively to the call for sacrifice, hard work and constructive contribution to their and their nation's development- a spirit which has come to be embodied in the philosophy of development called TESITO" (Government of The Gambia, 1980: 2). It defined *tesito* as "that spirit of individual and collective effort to improve one's lot in society as a whole." If *luta continua* ("the struggle continues") was the mobilizing force in Guinea-Bissau, in The Gambia, it was *tesito*. It was also incorporated through the formal educational system, where radio programs on the theme were made part of the school curriculum and broadcast during scheduled classes. These lessons had strong cultural components.

Followership legitimatized Jawara's leadership through collaborating to achieve his political vision and development goals. Followership was also keen on neutralizing his political rivals, who they saw as betrayers of the national cause. For example, women supporting Jawara made songs against P.S. Njie, to caricature his leadership, question his ethics, morals and practices. The lyrics of a Mandinka women's song denounced Njie as a betrayer in the terms below.

> *Yee*, Pierre Njie fled from you
> *Yee*, Pierre Njie abandoned you
> He went to the big Governor's place
> And wailed to him "can't you see the PPP people want to kill me"
> People of The Gambia, Pierre Njie fled from you
> He abandoned you…

The song cast Njie as a traitor unfit to lead the country. In Mandinka culture leaders stayed with their people during crisis. Hence, during war, a leader goes to the war front and an interim leadership takes over during his absence (see Chapter 1). Njie's leadership was questioned based on principles of Mandinka leadership culture and ethics. Sheriff Dibba, a Mandinka, and another political rival of Jawara, had his leadership condemned like Njie's (see Chapter 3). Therefore, it was understandable that Jawara insisted on returning to the country when political threats emerged during his international travels, like in 1981 when rebel forces tried to usurp power, and during the 22 July 1994 coup d'état, which toppled his regime. It was reported that on the day of the coup Jawara had to be begged to stay for safety on board the American marine vessel that docked near the state house. The most defeating lyrics women composed against P.S. Njie were:

> Barefoot Pierre Njie's Banjul odyssey
>
> The Wollof women of Banjul expelled him from their hotel
>
> This year, if he is not careful, he will perish of want and shame.

These lyrics imply solidarity with the Wollof women in Banjul who denounced and snubbed Njie, which resulted in serious psychological stress for him. He became a recluse in Banjul.

A Wollof phrase *"dafma Pierre Njie"* ("he/she has Pierre Njie me") was used to deride his political and social withdrawal following the political rejection. To this day, the phrase is used to mean snubbing someone. Women's lack of confidence in Njie's leadership became a popular metaphor for social snobbery.

The internalization of the *"balang"* (resistance) culture shaped anti-colonial resistance of the protectorate and non-Aku subjects of the colony, reflecting the *nyanchoo* spirit of fighting to the end. People from the protectorate used their cultural memory and indigenous art forms to mobilize against British colonial rule. At independence, they also used the same resources to entrench Jawara's leadership and to minimize the influences of his rivals. Jawara's politics directly borrowed from Mandinka history, culture and values, Cabral's was more indirect. Bissau-Guineans who rallied behind Cabral legitimized him as they employed different cultural strategies to win the war against Portugal. He is still remembered as the father of the nation, which reinforces the intergenerational legitimacy his memory has. Cabral believed the place of the party leaders should be among the populations. Unfortunately, the educational infrastructure that was necessary for building the right ideological foundation for a free Guinea-Bissau was not sustained after he was assassinated. The Mandinka had an entire occupational caste that appropriated the mission to excel in knowledge, become dependable service providers, and reliable individuals to successfully propagate and spread Mandinka values, principles and philosophies. By the time Cabral died, Guinea-Bissau did not have a similar luxury that would gallantly pass over the legacies, thoughts and values of the liberation struggle. Luis Cabral came to power after his brother Amilcar was assassinated. But he too was killed. These two developments hindered the sustaining of the sophisticated thinking and culture-based education the PAIGC initiated during the liberation war. However, Cabral's ideas are still respected and echoed in Guinea-Bissau.

Conclusion

The PPP in The Gambia and PAIGC in Guinea-Bissau used historical knowledge, cultural thought and strategies to develop counter-rhetoric and counter-strategies against the colonial state. Ethnicity was a resource and not a curse in their strategies. They successfully forged shared values and common visions for fighting and ending colonial domination. The transformations they achieved were modeled on some precolonial thoughts. However, the strategies were adapted to the colonial circumstances to show continuities and discontinuities that shaped anti-colonial activities. This was similar to how Kaabu adapted and changed some Manding practices to suit its circumstances. The changes can also be understood in relation to Acemoglu and Robinson's observation that Great Britain, the USA and other Western countries "became rich because their citizens overthrew the elites who controlled power and created a society where political rights were much more broadly distributed, where government was accountable and responsive to citizens, and where the great mass of people could take advantage of economic opportunities" (Acemoglu and Robinson, 2012: 3–4). The colonizer–colonized relation shifted toward new directions when African agency faced new constraints. Migdal (1988) asserted that Western social scientists directed the development of new African states like The Gambia and Guinea-Bissau, seeking to improve their state capacities. But this venture had limited success. Consequently, scholars like Herbst (2000) think colonial rule was not the problem. Rather, African territories had huge control of land, and less people. This made it difficult for them to provide basic public goods, law and order, enforce contracts or build infrastructure like a normal state should. But the length of Kaabu's statehood provides examples of viable precolonial states. Additionally, the political and cultural memories the colonized drew from to liberate themselves proved they had a strong history of political courage, vision and strategies. The growing scarcity of land in countries like The Gambia, which is beset by a plethora of land-related disputes in the urban areas, the increasing demands citizens are making on the state to act as a state, indicate claim-makings about moral politics that have cultural roots in indigenous social, cultural and political systems. These demands question the technical expertise that was designed to build the new African states (also see Tilly, 1990). As we will see in Chapter 3, the strategies of the anti-colonial movements were abandoned especially from the 1970s. The moral reservoirs that made them a success were eroded leading to a postcolonial political culture that instigates *maruf* politics and supports an abusive political, leadership and followership culture. Hence, Justice, Truth and Integrity movements are now demanding responsibility from the state, and a new political and institutional culture. Moreover, these demands are couched within the cultural history of society, as will be explored in Chapter 3.

References

Acemoglu, Daron and James A. Robinson. 2012. *The Origins of Power, Prosperity and Poverty, Why Nations Fail.* New York: Currency.

Africa Information Service. 1973. *Return to the Source: Selected Speeches of Amilcar Cabral.* New York and London: Monthly Review Press.

Cabral, Amilcar. 1979. *Unity and Struggle. Speeches and Writings of Amilcar Cabral. Monthly Review Press Classics.* Guinea-Bissau: PAIGC.

Chabal, Patrick. 2009. *Africa, The Politics of Suffering and Smiling.* London/New York: Zed Books.

Drammeh, Oko. 2014. "Gambia's mighty Jazz drummer of the Ifangbondi Band." *Bantaba in Cyberspace Gambia.* 31 January.

Dunayeskaya, Raya. 1962. "In the Gambia during Elections." *Africa Today*, 9(6), 12–15.

Ekeh, P. Peter. 1975. "Colonialism and the Two Publics in Africa: A Theoretical Statement" *Comparative Studies in Society and History*, 17(1), 91–112.

Government of The Gambia. 1980. *The Gambia Since Independence: 1965–1980, Fifteen Years of Nationhood*, 1–15.

Hannoum, Abdelmajid. 2016. *Practicing Sufism: Sufi Politics and Performance, 1st edition.* New York: Routledge.

Havik, Philip J. 2009. "Motor cars and modernity: Pinning for Progress in Portuguese Guinea, 1915-1945." In *The Speed of Change, Motor Vehicles in Africa, 1890-2000*, edited by Jan-Bart Gewald, Sabing Luning and Klaas van Walraven, pp. 48–74. Leiden: Brill.

Herbst, Jeffrey I. 2000. *States and Power in Africa: Comparative Lessons in Authority and Control.* Princeton, NJ: Princeton University Press.

Holcombe, Susan H. 2021. Email to author, 24 March.

Huxley, Elspeth. 1954 quoted in Baldeh, 2014, "The Gambia in the 1950s," *The Standard Newspaper*, 2 May 2014.

Kandel, Matt. 2015. "Politics from below? Small-, mid- and large-scale land dispossession in Teso, Uganda, and the relevance of scale." *Journal of Peasant Studies*, 42(3–4), 635–652.

Karibe Mendy, Peter. 2020. Interview with author, 10 August.

Khan, Mariama. 2014. "Indigenous Languages and Africa's Development Dilemma." *Journal of Development in Practice (DiP)*, 764–776.

Khan, Mariama (unpublished). "How threats to entitlements, ethnicity, minority nationalism, Casamance rebellion and Structural Adjustment collapsed the Senegambia Confederation, 1982–1989."

Ly, Aliou. (2014). "Promise and betrayal: women fighters and national liberation in Guinea-Bissau." *Feminist Africa*, 19, 24–42.

Mamdani, Mahmood. 2018. *Citizen and Subject, Contemporary Africa and the Legacy of Late Colonialism. With a new Preface by the Author*. Princeton, NJ and Oxford: Princeton University Press.

Migdal, Joel. S. 1988. *Strong Societies and Weak States: State-Society Relations and State Capabilities in the Third World*. Princeton, NJ: Princeton University Press.

Mwakikagile, Godfrey. 2010. *The Gambia and Its People, Ethnic Identities and Cultural Integration in Africa*. Dar es Salam: New Africa Press.

Sallah, Tijan M. 2021. *Saani Baat, Aspects of African Literature and Culture*. Trenton, NJ: Africa World Press.

Tilly, Charles. 1990. *Coercion, Capitalism and European States, AD 990-1990*. Malden: Blackwell Publishers.

Vieira, João Bernardo. 2020. Interview with author, 17 and 19 July.

3   Tumbling political visions

> Diverse tribal groups should work at achieving unity by stressing
> nationality, not tribe. A united Gambia has to be part of the process of
> building-up a peaceful nation.
>
> (Bishop Michael Cleary, quoted in Gambia Daily, 1996a)

> All big things end in a small way
>
> (A Mandinka proverb)

The early phases of Sir Dawda Jawara's postcolonial leadership in The
Gambia formally recognized that Kaabu was a strong cultural influence on The Gambia. The *kora*, a Mandinka musical instrument,
was adopted as an important national cultural symbol. The country's
national anthem "For The Gambia Our Homeland" was rendered using
Foday Kaba, a traditional *kora* melody. The anthem itself reflected several traditional Mandinka values and concerns during their respective
state-building endeavors in West Africa. It implied the national vision
and embodied themes of national discourses and aspirations, which
resonated with traditional Mandinka political and social views. For
example, the "homeland" concept in the opening lines of the anthem,
"For The Gambia, Our homeland, We Strive, Work And Pray" was
integral to Mandinka culture, history and inter-generational pledge
(see Introduction and Chapter 1). Throughout Jawara's early postcolonial leadership, he appealed to and praised the "hardwork" (*sobeya*)
and "sacrifice" of Gambians. Furthermore, the anthem fittingly paid
homage to God and spirituality, the common good, freedom (*forooya*),
justice (*tilingho*), unity and trust (*lanno*) and loyalty to The Gambia. It
invoked the concerns and values that shaped the anti-colonial struggles
of the PPP (People's Progressive Party). Thus, the national anthem
reproduced longstanding yearnings for a solid nation. "Peace, Progress

DOI: 10.4324/9781003140009-4

and Prosperity" became the national motto and its emblem, the two hoes, depicted the importance of farming to local communities from precolonial to colonial times.

Other *kora* tunes like *Cheddo*, *Alpha Yahya*, *Kelephaba*, *Masanneh Ceesay*, *Yundumunku* and *Bamba Bojang* were integrated into the nation's cultural fabric. *Cheddo* is a tune that pays homage to *nyanchoo* values and history. The rest of these traditional songs celebrate warriors, personalities, kings, and chiefs who played legendary roles in Kabunka and Gambian histories. Their memories were celebrated in oral histories and folklore. Mai Fatty, current leader of the Gambia Moral Congress (GMC), adopted the moniker *"dingdin mansa,"* a title given to Kelephaba, a Kabunka prince reputed for his extraordinary skills and leadership qualities. His community declared him *"dingdin mansa"* (youth king) when his uncle was still on the throne to celebrate his charisma and knowledge (see Chapter 1). ST, the popular Brikama-born Afro-Manding rapper uses the same moniker.

Like the precolonial Kabunka and Manding leaders, Jawara had a personal *jali*. Other famous *jalis* like Nyama Suso, Bai Conteh, Faballah Kuyateh, Suntu Suso, Alaji Kunye Suso and Amadou Bansang Jobarteh became national icons. The Gambia was declared a "center of Manding culture" (Government of the Gambia, 1980: 43–44) and many Mandinka social customs were observed. In times of reckoning, these *jalis* played true to their status and spoke truth to power.

Street corner dances like *lenjeng* became common in both urban and rural areas. Dance rituals in *lenjeng* preserved social relations. Dancers deferred to each other in the dance circle by bending double to the side, clapping for the one in the circle or curtseying to older dancers. Older dancers paid homage to the younger ones by removing their head-tie – a social ritual employed to acknowledge someone (as used during a dance), to beg for forgiveness or to curse an individual. *Lenjeng* was an entertainment with political utility. It promoted social patience and respect and entrenched local traditions and customs in society.

The PPP aimed to build a cultural infrastructure that would preserve, restore and revitalize The Gambia's cultural heritage and history. The department of cultural affairs was established in 1973–1974 and it held its first National Festival of Arts and Culture. Traditional Mandinka society was known to organize events for its youths to demonstrate their skills, character, reputation or gaming powers. The first national youth week and cultural festival organized by the PPP emulated that spirit. The cultural revival taking place in the country was noticeable by 1980.

Other historical yearnings in Mandinka history, like environmental sustainability, which was enshrined and protected in the 1236 Manden charter and in the later histories of Mandinka communities, were invoked when Jawara signed the 1977 Banjul Declaration to protect the flora and fauna of The Gambia. Posters of the declaration were widely circulated within the country. People hang them in houses, in shops and in any other places they can have them. An opposition party like PDOIS, currently led by Halifa Sallah, and which had multi-ethnic founders, tilted toward Mandinka cultural values. It named its newspaper *Forooyaa* (the Mandinka term for "freedom" but also "character").

The kinds of social, cultural and political consolidation that happened in The Gambia was not achieved in Guinea-Bissau following Cabral's assassination. The country became liberated in 1973. President Luis Cabral, who took over from his brother Amilcar, was overthrown by prime minister General João Bernardo Vieira on 14 November 1980. The ideology of the African Party for the Independence of Guinea and Cape Verde (PAIGC), which was passed on to members through internal lectures, seminar discussions "guides to actions" and "operational orders" established a strong foundation to achieve freedom. The education, which included developing technical capabilities such as knowing parts of the helicopter, fixing guns and carrying them, and multiple other skills necessary for the struggle, everyday events and life itself, was robust enough but needed to be sustained in postcolonial Guinea-Bissau for a successful achievement of the maximum program (see Chapter 2). The power of ideology and truth-telling was equally popularized. Under Cabral, the study of reality at home became a basis for "a theory of effective action for determined ends" (Cabral, 1979: xii). But PAIGC's founding visions were not sustained for long in post-Amilcar Cabral Guinea-Bissau. Cabral's "new society" project faced a leadership struggle. The longstanding tension between the Cape Verdean and Bissau-Guinean leaders, which was neutralized under him, grew intense. This frustrated the postwar national reconstruction effort. The country's socialist development strategy was marred by persistent political crisis and worsening economic conditions.

This chapter explores the trends and discontinuities between early postcolonial Gambia and Bissau-Guinean politics and Kabunka and Manding leadership, followership and nation-building values and practices. It highlights how modern political culture evolved from the past and how colonial and postcolonial economic, social and political legacies shape current political understandings and culture. The main question it answers is: how did the precolonial experience interact with colonial rule to transform postcolonial political culture in The Gambia and Guinea-Bissau? It looks at how the yearnings for the past depict moral reservoirs that encapsulate visions of justice, morality, freedom and development. It also explores how these visions get subverted and the impact of such subversions, as keenly reflected in the current demands Justice, Truth and Integrity movements (JITs) are making on the state.

This introduction is followed by a discussion of how political visions are contested. After that I discuss how political rhetoric relates to general social and political culture and practice. This is followed by the conclusion.

Contested political futures

The Gambianization policy the PPP adopted in 1959 in response to the colonial government's "Africanization" policy in The Gambia guided Jawara's policies at early independence (see Chapter 2). The government's immediate concerns were international solvency and economic independence. However, that did not obstruct its Gambianization agenda, which started with the replacement of expatriate staff with Gambian officials. By 1966, government departments, like the Accountant-General's, Customs, Education (except Yundum College), Labour, Lands Office, Printing, Prisons and Surveys, were completely Gambianized. Jawara being a man of moderation, the policy did not aim to completely eradicate expatriate staff in government. There were still a significant number of expatriate staff in the country and at Yundum College in 1980 (Gambia Daily, 1996b: 8). There were similar institutional adjustments in other sectors of the administration. The dual administrative system that existed under colonial rule was unified. However, the use of district officers (commissioners) and chiefs to govern the protectorate (now provinces) was maintained. Other representative local government institutions were devised to promote both urbanization and rural development. To improve rural–urban connectivity, the ship *Lady Wright* sailed weekly between the provinces and Banjul. Later, the country owned a second ship *Bintang Bolong*, which sailed between Banjul and the UK. Radio Gambia, which was newly set up, broadcast news in English and local languages, which became another important means of connecting rural and urban communities, as different public information on obituaries, cultural and religious events were announced on the radio. The programming on Radio Gambia reinforced the status of English as the official language and the language of government business, in continuation of the colonial government's language policy.

The Gambianization policy led to an important monetary policy decision in 1971, the introduction of the dalasis, The Gambia's own currency, in place of the colonial shilling (British Pound sterling). This was an important break from the colonial legacy. It was stabilized and it performed very well against major international currencies. In 1971, the exchange rate between the British pound sterling and dalasi was one pound to five dalasis.

The zeal to prove wrong skeptics of Gambian statehood was high. The government adopted a liberal economic policy that boosted its re-export trade as cheap goods imported into the country were reexported to neighboring states. The Jawara government's development vision envisaged a developed agricultural sector, diversification and encouragement of new industries, sound economical administration, provision of employment, fair distribution of income and economic activities between Banjul and the provinces based on prudent financial management and administrative practice, and improved livestock and fisheries sectors. However, its agricultural policy retained its colonial influence. Women continued to grow rice and engaged in market gardening. Men grew millet and groundnuts. Cooperative societies continued to work with the produce-buying markets, retaining a key structure of the colonial economy. More importantly, the government sought to establish law and order and peaceful climate for trade and commerce. Some of the colonial institutional systems were maintained; where necessary, there was some reversal to existing colonial set-ups.

Jawara broke away from the colonial vision for the country when he adopted the "Singapore dream" as the national aspiration. This was a significant redefinition of the national goal. But the model it aspired to follow was informed by geography and other realities of the country. His ambitions in politics and development did not, however, inflate his ego. He remained a modest man who defined himself as a servant of the people. He stated that "To be in politics provides one with an opportunity to serve one's people ... to be a Minister only means that one is a servant." Therefore, his role was "to provide the necessary leadership and to enlist the services of all the people." In the minds of the ordinary people, he was a unifier and a non-tribal leader. His temperament endeared him to the majority of Gambians, and that helped to destabilize the support-base of political parties that rivalled PPP. For example, in 1966, the United Party (UP) had eight seats against PPP's 24 in the assembly. By 1972, Jawara captured four seats from the UP, giving him 28 seats. It was believed his personality and temperament contributed to this victory. According to a retired Gambian politician: "During Sir Dawda Jawara's first election from Pakaliba to Fuladu , Fatoto to Fuladu were all UP. But when elections were held he won ... He exercised *sabaro* (patience) to pull those UP people to him and this was what united the country" (Manneh, 2020). There was mutual trust between him and ordinary citizens. They praised his qualities but he also proudly applauded some of what he considered as the intrinsic qualities of Gambian people such as the "orderly nature of our people," which to him can importantly contribute to peace and stability in the continent. He extolled the virtues of tolerance, understanding and friendliness of Gambians as other important values that would contribute to the government's overall goal, which was to bring "an improved standard of living to all Gambians." Jawara's image of Gambian virtues was very different from the colonial image of Gambians as rebellious.

The big flaw in Jawara's noble agenda was that, instead of vigorously exploring ways to diversify and sustainably build the economy, the ambitious plan was dependent on the "goodwill of friendly nations" (Government of The Gambia, 1980, 1–15). In other words, his development plans rested on a donor-driven economy. Another serious flow was that the pursuit of *londoo* (education/knowledge), which was an important Mandinka preoccupation in ancient Mali and other Mandinka dominions, became illusive. His government, like the colonial government, made negligible investment in education and training. These were required to develop the necessary skillsets that could successfully transform the country and achieve the "Singapore dream." The low investment in education would be an important factor in alienating youth from Jawara's government.

One of the most significant events to shake the Jawara government's public reputation was the 1972 butut scandal. The brother of Sheriff Mustapha Dibba, vice president, was implicated in a fraudulent scheme, in which bututs, the smallest denomination of Gambian currency, were smuggled to Dakar, Senegal, and transformed into jewelry. Dibba resigned as vice president, but later formed the National People's Party (NCP).

Another event that rocked the PPP's reputation was the Saul Samba–Matarr Sarr incident, which arose out of the legacies of the clientelist colonial commercial relations in Bathurst. Sarkis Madi, a prominent Lebano-Syrian had been, since 1940, the colonial government's favorite. He served in the colonial legislative council for 17 years and was the chairman of the Chamber of Commerce for 23 years. By 1965, his company had business interests in every sector of the Gambian economy. Senior officials of the Jawara government, top politicians in the country, senior civil servants and police officials, had credit accounts with Madi's. Matarr Sarr and Saul Samba were two friends who served together in the colonial police service. At an early age, Sarr rose through the ranks and became its second most senior Gambian official. He later resigned and joined Madi's, where he became the most senior of the Gambian staff and was in charge of the company's accounts. He decided to quit in 1971 to create his own insurance and shipping company. Madi's recruited Gambian officials, among them Lamin Saho, then Attorney General and Minister of Justice, Harry Evans, then Chief of Police, Sam George, then Chief Justice, and other senior officials in government, to eliminate Sarr and end the expansion of his businesses. Unfortunately, Sarr's ex-wife was married to Saho. This became an interpersonal complication between him and the attorney general, and did not help in his commercial rivalry with Madi's. Without any notice, the government suspended Sarr's companies, leading to his clients' fury toward him. Clients besieged him, he sought clarification from the government on why his companies' operations had been halted. He was advised to see Attorney General Saho. But when Sarr went to his office, Saho summoned the police to arrest him for alleged "criminal trespassing." He was taken to court before Mr Amanda, a Ceylonese-born magistrate. On 1 April 1972, he was released on bail. Sarr was requested to appear in court again but refused. Saul Samba, his best friend and former colleague in the police force, was asked to arrest him but he was killed in the process. In March 1973, along Pipeline Road in Fajara, heavily armed members of The Gambia police force and the paramilitary field force troops barricaded a house to shoot down Matarr Sarr. After eight hours of constant exchange of gun fire, his bullet ridden body was removed from his residence (Manjang, 1983; Touray, 2014).

This incident shocked Gambians. But it showed the force of the clientelist commercial relations that existed from colonial times to Jawara's rule. It also reminded of stories of misguided love affairs and triangles that embarrassed the colonial government – the most high-profile of which was the love affair between a provincial woman Fatou Khan and a British colonial official. Under Jawara's rule, such affairs continued with officials sometimes snatching each other's wives, leading to intense interpersonal conflicts that seeped into their professional and family lives.

The early 1970s proved to be a testing time for Jawara's government. The 1973 Arab oil embargo, which caused a worldwide recession, seriously affected developing countries like The Gambia and Guinea-Bissau. The Gambia, like Guinea-Bissau, had to implement the structural adjustments prescribed by the World Bank and International Monetary Fund (IMF). These economic recovery plans were defective policy packages that led to massive retrenchments, the withdrawing of social services, increased international debt burdens and general social hardship in the adjusting countries (see Mkandawire and Soluda,

1999). Moreover, the legacy of colonial government corruption became entrenched in both The Gambia and Guinea-Bissau.

As the global economic recession and the effects of structural adjustment tightened in The Gambia of the late 1970s, Jawara's previous approach to development shifted. *Tesito* (see Chapter 2) and the "Singapore dream" became mere rhetoric. The government's new focus was on "national reconstruction." Its agenda was tailored to fit external expectations, serving the growing international debt, implementing externally generated ideas of poverty alleviation, empowering women, etc., based on what were considered as international best practices at the time. The government continued to neglect the development of the technological and industrial base of the economy. It also moved away from its initial efforts to ground the state within collective Gambian cultural experiences.

By 1980, Gambian youth still had limited access to education, training and self-development. They were frustrated, especially youth in Banjul. Those who came of age by 1980 were described as "violent and aggressive 'ndongos'" who constituted "a permanently unemployed generation of youngsters, breed in shashas-smoking, palm wine drinking, street fighting, and knife jabbing," and were making Gambia a tough rough society (Manjang, 1983; Touray, 2014). Gambian youths turned to Marxism, with many of them becoming members of the Movement for Justice in Africa (MOJA), which had a Gambian chapter, MOJA-G. They expressed their frustrations through graffiti-making and the writing of slogans on walls and public spaces. There was no doubt that some of these youth were super bright as they shared their Marxist views with others.

The youth and their Marxist supporters accused the government of rampant corruption – some officials of the Jawara government were increasingly notorious for allegedly demanding sexual favors from desperate Gambian women looking for jobs, scholarships or other government benefits for them, their children or other family members. They called for a change of government. The Supreme National Revolutionary Council, headed by Kukoi Samba Sanyang, attempted a civilian-led overthrow of Jawara's government in 1981. But international goodwill and Senegalese military intervention helped quash the rebellion, though with significant human and material cost. There was looting of businesses, many deaths and random detention and arrest of people either because they were believed to have participated in the rebellion or their family members had. This memory informed some future actions of the Jammeh government, which employed similar tactics during times of crisis. The rebellion also set the tone of future political rhetoric and the use of nakedness as a political weapon in Gambian politics. Pictures of ill-clad people under arrest or being paraded shocked the public eye.

As the country reeled from the effects of the rebellion, the *jalis* resorted to oral art to ensure Jawara's democratic habits were not derailed by the shock of the rebellion. They composed the following lyrics to counsel him: "DK [Dawda Kairaba] be patient / Kukoi ran, DK be patient." Sulayman Sanyang, a former Gambian photojournalist, noted that "Jawara's supporters came up with the song to calm him down to ease the pressure of mass arrests. It was a short and powerful message, ... a way of speaking truth to power. It asked him to compromise with The Gambia" (Sanyang, 2020). The Mandinka *jalis'* short but powerful public rebuttal of the excesses of the Jawara government following the rebellion indicated that the *jali* still maintained their traditional status as speakers of truth to power, protectors of freedom and the common good. This song can be contrasted to early songs in which the *jali* deployed their oral skills to offset the popularity and power of Jawara's political rivals.

Following the fall-out with vice president Sheriff Dibba over the butut scandal, the *jali* rushed to Jawara's defense and questioned Dibba's character and political intentions. The following biting lyrics were a frontal assault on him: "Shame on him, *Nkunja* [catfish, nickname for Sheriff Dibba] is coming / Sheriff Dibba / You and your followers and your flags / PPP has beaten you." The use of the *Nkunja* moniker implied Dibba was taken away from the government like the catfish is fished out of sea. Traditionally, the catfish is smoked before it is cooked. That implies Sheriff Dibba was politically dead and burnt. He could never make a political comeback. The flag symbolizes rising, but for him there cannot be such since PPP was towering above it. The lyrics of another anti-Sheriff Dibba song condemned political anger and corruption:

My friends, the youths, Sheriff Dibba is fooling you

The marabouts are fooling him

They are extorting huge sums of money from him, it is just wastage

He is exhausting himself with goings and comings and buying fuel for his car

You see, he was butted out of this government because of stealing

The shame of stealing and anger has made them form a new party

The angry people met and had a conversation

The troublemakers met and said let's have a conversation
Let's form our party to remove *Mansa* [referring to Jawara] from power
They do not know what they are doing
Removing *Mansa* is beyond them.

The essence of these lyrics was similar to those sang earlier against P.S. Njie (see Chapter 2). The song disparages Dibba's character and says he was untrustworthy and youth should be wary of him and his party. It emphasizes that anger is destructive and it is not a quality a good leader should exhibit and use to shape his decisions. The song more importantly addresses a pervasive cultural practice in which people who want to become leaders consult marabouts for them to employ their occult knowledge to make them leaders. For the song, being a leader is a natural gift and an endowment from God, not marabouts. The song is more than three decades old, but it captures the spirit of President Adama Barrow's recent nationally stunning discourse about the use of marabouts to get to leadership. In July 2021, President Barrow revealed in an interview that when he was a member of the United Democratic Party (UDP), they were consulting marabouts to make the lawyer Ousainou Darboe president. At one point, a marabout gave them three charms and they had to open graves at the cemetery to put them there. In the political fall-out between NPP and UDP, it appears the statement was intended to expose the purported "dark side" of the UDP and its leadership. But this was a self-incriminating revelation which the government needed to investigate since it desecrates death and public cemeteries.

Songs were also used to predict political futures. The following lyrics express the implications of political rejection. As the Banjul women did to P.S. Njie, the song indicates Sheriff Dibba was also rejected by the community of Jambangjelly and therefore he and his party had failed: "NCP wooo, NCP failed / Jambangjelly said you will not enter their community." These lyrics can be contrasted with the lyrics of this pro-Jawara song: "The Mansa of good times… / President Jawara treats all people equally / Mansa of good times / Who celebrates his people… / Have you not hear that Jawara has taken the mantle of leadership in this land." These lines joyously respond to Jawara's celebration of Gambian people by celebrating him, his character and leadership qualities to further legitimize him. Overall, anti-Sheriff Dibba songs, like the anti-P.S.Njie songs, were prophetic – Dibba never became president.

Songs were composed to support or condemn leadership and to express political visions and perceptions of the political system or society. For example, the women in the following lyrics present other forms of literacy that give them legitimacy to participate in national politics: "Do not take me fore-granted because I sing / I am equal to the educated ones / I have memorised the *fatiha* [which means the opening Surah of the Quran] / I know the letters of the Arabic alphabet." The song implicitly toes Jawara's development philosophy, which states that all Gambians have something to contribute toward the country's development. It reinvokes pride in singing, the *jali* and *finna*'s role in society, and access to spiritual/religious education, in this case Islam. But irrespective of the public trust that Jawara enjoyed, and how well he was celebrated by *jalis* of the country, the *jalis* thought his government's reaction in the aftermath of the 1981 rebellion was over the top and therefore publicly called him out on that. The crisis had a serious impact on Jawara's political views and visions. He hastily established a confederation with Senegal in 1982. By 1989, the tense Senegambia confederation collapsed, causing frosty Gambia–Senegal interstate relations (see Khan, 2019).

The PPP government instituted a commission of enquiry to investigate the rebellion. During sittings of the commission, some people who looted businesses voluntarily returned the items they took. This development indicated that public or social and individual morality were still appreciated in society. Such acts echoed a longstanding social moral practice in which, when people possess materials that were deemed to be beyond their means, they would be questioned by their parents or other family members about the source.

Notwithstanding, public corruption existed within the ranks of the PPP government. Some observers think that the effects of structural adjustment contributed to eroding social morals. Somerville studied the effects adjustment had on Dakar and concluded that it led to reliance on exported goods and services, the development of interpersonal interests based on material self-interest and money, the degradation of family relations and friendships, the greater exhibition of individualistic, opportunistic behavior, and a decline in solidarity and tradition (see Somerville 1991: 63). Structural Adjustment Programs (SAP) according to the finding promoted a moral crisis in the adjusting crisis. It was under these circumstances that, in 1994, the Jawara government imposed user fees on public water facilities in Brikama. This was part of the prescriptions from structural adjustment. Women in Brikama revolted against the government. Singing *"jeyu, jeyu, mokana jiyu san"* ("water, water, no one must buy water"), they went around town attracting support for their plight. On 22 July 1994, "young officers of the Gambia National Army staged a military coup and deposed Jawara"

(Khan, 2016: 82). The Armed Forces Provisional Ruling Council (AFPRC), headed by 29-year-old Captain Yahya Jammeh, came to power with "accountability," "transparency" and "probity," their rhetoric. This instantly resonated with the youth. By 1996, Jammeh became a civilian president.

Similar to The Gambia, Guinea-Bissau started an economic stabilization/recovery program by March 1983. It started implementing structural adjustment by 1987, which negatively affected the agricultural sector. "The privatization of public assets made a few members of the political, military, and administrative elites very rich" but the social costs were massive. Healthcare and education sectors further deteriorated (Karibe Mendy, 2020).

The persistent political tensions and instability in the country affected the social landscape as the military became politicized, various institutions of government suffered serious decay, and the legislature became dysfunctional. Political reforms in 1994 led to multi-party elections, but the political situation remained turbulent. Respective governments struggled to complete their constitutional mandates.

Pierre Englebert, then a staff of the World Bank, worked with the Bissau-Guinean government in 1990. He recalled his impressions of the country:

> Guinea-Bissau struck me as being in the weak end in terms of infrastructure. It was very poor ... compared to Burkina Faso, Burkina was poor, there was a sense of poverty, but there was also a sense of people coming together to make things happen ... but the state in Guinea-Bissau was disconnected from the people and people were left much to their own means.
>
> (Englebert, 2020)

The political and social situation in Guinea-Bissau was bleak, to the extent that "as the World Bank we have to embrace this discourse that you can develop ... but no one really believed that there was a foundation to engineer transformation" (Englebert, 2020). For Englebert, Guinea-Bissau's problems included the fact that the country did not have the requisite human capital to engineer the diversification of its economy to achieve the necessary economic transformation the country needed. The country's export revenue came from cashew nuts, which is about 90% of the national revenue. But one could not build a state on cashew nuts without diversification. Englebert's view of the country's leadership at the time of his visits was that "a gang controlled the state, a bunch of different people then start their own gangs ... drug smuggling became a big thing." There was what Bayart (2009) called a "criminal state, a state whose actors use the tool of sovereignty to engage in entrepreneurial criminal activities … it makes sense when there is something little going on it triggers an environment of violence, it further erodes the state." João Bernardo Vieira (2020) views that the war of independence seriously affected the country. It left many people with a war mindset. This is partly why the military always intervened in politics.

The killing of the two Cabral brothers prematurely cut off the cycle of social and political transformation that had started during the liberation war. The minimum and maximum programs were conceptually impressive and, if they had been fully implemented, perhaps could have helped to bring out the necessary social and psychological transformation to erase war mentalities and replace them with those for peace. The hopeless political situation brought to the fore the ethnic sentiments that were suppressed during the liberation war.

If the state is not addressing what it should address, people step in to find ways of addressing it. The oral arts have been appropriated by people to express their political dissatisfactions and visions. There are some Mandinka/Kriol songs that refer to the fight of Amilcar Cabral and everything he did for Guinea-Bissau. The lyrics of one such song states, "wherever you go in the world, they say Guinea-Bissau, who did that … *Bartaba, Bartaba*." The words "*Bartaba, Bartaba*" refer to Amilcar Cabral. The song pays homage to his work. It expresses nostalgia about his leadership in the face of the struggling leadership Guinea-Bissau has endured since independence. Song-making to express political visions is an important political act in the country. People make songs to describe past and current political situations. They make songs about the lack of electricity, about instability, lack of quality education, schools and about other notions important to them. The oral arts therefore provide important avenues for expressing political visions, moral concerns and social aspirations in both The Gambia and Guinea-Bissau.

The next section explores political rhetoric, legitimacy and song-making in the more recent political histories of both The Gambia and Guinea-Bissau. The section also shows how political culture evolves as it reclaims or subverts ideas from previous regimes.

Political rhetoric and legitimacy: post-1994 to 2021

Yahya Jammeh came to power in 1994 through a coup d'état that vilified Jawara-era politics. When he transitioned into a civil president in 1996, his mimicry of Jawara-era politics showed. When colonial rule ended, Jawara's government used rhetoric about "cultural and social reorientation," as fundamental to eliminating the colonial daze from Gambian society. Subsequently, it added "national reconstruction" to its rhetorical toolbox in response to the 1970s economic shock. Jammeh's political party, the Alliance for Patriotic Reorientation and Construction (APRC), repurposed those ideas to reflect them in the name of the party. It retained "reorientation," but dropped the "re" in reconstruction, and maintained "construction." By 1996, decentralization, governance and sustainable development were also buzzwords of the APRC government. These examples show how political rhetoric is sometimes carried over from one regime to another. But there were obvious breaks between Jawara's approach to leadership and Jammeh's.

Jawara enjoyed massive support among the elders and women. When Jammeh came to power as a military leader, he courted the youth and women to legitimize his rule. As his power waned, he foraged into religious circles to reactivate his legitimacy by declaring The Gambia an Islamic state, toward the end of his regime. Similarly, under President Adama Barrow some UDP and NPP supporters equally use ethnic cards to legitimize and attract support for their respective leaders as the December 2021 election approached. Jammeh's action resonated with the notion of evolutionary legitimacy as he explored new enclaves of political support, in this case from certain critical pockets of the majority Muslim population, to repackage his political appeal. In essence, the move was similar to former President Chiluba's 1991 declaration of Zambia as a Christian nation to appease the majority Christian population of the country.

Realistically, Jammeh's declaration had no pure intent to turn The Gambia into an Islamic state as feared by some parts of the Gambian Christian community and the international community. It was a mere attempt to re-create political legitimacy for a regime that was fast approaching its end. It was also another way of re-creating a social contract for the relegitimization of a regime on life-support. Later, in 2016, Jammeh lost the elections to President Adama Barrow.

Political rhetoric under Jammeh developed interesting dimensions, demonstrating his political skills. As he transitioned from a military leader to a civilian president, his rhetoric mirrored those of the religious leaders: Ahmadis, Christians and Muslims. His initial self-endearing rhetoric, such as declarations about zero tolerance for corruption, laziness in the civil service and support for merit, a "definitive no to drugs" policy all resonated with society. His rhetoric evolved to demonstrate his awareness of the need to entrench his legitimacy in all corners of society. Thus, messages like attitudinal change and zero tolerance for corruption were repackaged and repurposed to suit the country's Vision 2020 aspiration. Vision 2020 was the Jammeh version of Jawara's "Singapore dream." In reality, there was significant corruption in the country and the rhetoric about attitudinal change did not go far in the civil service. Attitudinal change, which is still an important theme in Gambian political discourses, captures concerns about social and political morality. A decent society is the fruit of decent families, decent people, decent communities. But both social and political decency were not a given. Jammeh's use of traditional motifs of power further popularized his rule. He gave national status to *Futampaf*, a traditional Jola initiation ceremony, which made him a protector of Jola values. Whether invented or real, he declared descent from *mansa* Mama Tamba Jammeh, an important king in Baddibu. This would later be the basis of the campaign to declare him *mansa* of The Gambia. But when demands of democracy obstructed the *mansa* project, some key Jammeh supporters conceived with the president and popularized the notion "*baabili mansa*" ("the king that bridges rivers"). The image of the presidency was constantly repacked during Jammeh's rule. He adopted the speaking patterns of some traditional leaders, including those from *nyanchoo* backgrounds. He also adopted a white *waramba* dress code befitting religious and respectable traditional leaders in Gambian culture. The dress code symbolized a leader that was wise, reliable, truthful and mature. The staff and the book he carried in public were all symbols taken from traditional leadership motifs. The monikers people close to him used for him were connected with how his dress and rhetoric evolved. For example, *oga* (a term borrowed from Nigeria) implied in Gambian usage the wealthy, but flamboyant, patronizing boss who does what suits him. This name was used in relation to his military leadership. But *pabe*, which supplanted *oga*, was a respectable Wollof term used for elderly people, including revered religious personalities. The "*nasiru-al- deen*" title given to Jammeh was an extension of the *pabe* image.

The attribution of solid Islamic knowledge and piety to Jammeh informed his undiscerning decision to declare The Gambia an Islamic state, which roused Christian religious sensibilities. Image-building became an important part of Jammeh's presidency, which political opportunists capitalized on. In one song of praise, he was called "*nyanchoo la nyachooo*" ("royal warrior of royal warriors"). This was a direct reference to Kaabu's history.

Jammeh reproduced or subverted certain attitudes, metaphors or communication styles associated with Kaabu's history. The subversion of cultural motifs show how political discourses carry specific social concerns about leadership, followership, power and authority. Usually, such discourses employ cultural or social metaphors. The use of references such as "Baabili Mansa," a controversial moniker the use of which survived the post Jammeh presidency, indicates a yearning for a leadership that can achieve extraordinary feats for society. Acts like establishing the University of The Gambia were significant in the light of the educational needs of The Gambia. In traditional Mandinka society, such titles were given to leaders to measure the magnitude of some legendary achievements. Jammeh supporters devised the title to aggrandize his ego. It was also an indirect reclaiming of his contested descent from traditional Mandinka royalty. Jammeh also made use of *nyanchoo* culture in unrestrained political speeches through swearing/ cursing, and the use of inciteful words. This was very similar to Sanna B. Sabally's appropriation of *nyanchoo* culture during his leadership in the military council.

Sanna was among the young army captains who deposed Jawara's government on 22 July 1994. He became AFPRC's vice chairman and the secretary of state for the interior. All Gambians feared "Might Sabally," as he was infamously called during his brief erratic catapult to power. Some Gambians believed he had a special passion for *tajiriya*, the policy Janky Wally advocated in Kaabu. Sanna physically assaulted and tortured people. He spared no one – drivers on the roads, youths hanging out on the streets, women struggling in town for their survival, and even old people trying to get by in peace.

Shortly before he crashed from power, the national grapevine shared that he viciously slapped an old man in Basse, the Upper River Region. The abused old man warned him that he would be the last person he would ever slap in his life. Shortly after, on 27 January 1995, Sanna's fellow APRC junta members arrested him. Gambians sighed with relief at the news. Many people celebrated his arrest.

Recalling his brutal flirting with power during his testimony to the Truth, Reconciliation and Reparation Commission (TRRC; see Introduction), remorseless Sanna declared: "I am appealing to Gambians to forgive me. I was a young person without experience." His testimony divided Gambian public opinion. For some, the lead counsel of the TRRC, Essa Faal, treated Sanna like a hero as he recounted the horrific crimes he and his fellow AFPRC partners perpetrated against mostly innocent and peace-loving Gambians. For many, the TRRC gave a heartless criminal who deserved to be jailed for many horrendous crimes against innocent Gambians, an opportunity to cleanse himself before a previously antagonistic public opinion. Irrespective of the controversies around his testimony, Sanna's unrepentant body language and the bravado demonstrated during his TRRC testimony imitated outlandish *nyanchoo* discourse styles associated with some rogue leaders of Kaabu.

This brings us to the nature of political conversations under Jammeh and in contemporary Gambian society. One major effect of Jammeh's presidency is the widespread use of aggravated speech to express political or social dissatisfaction. Jawara responded to critics by borrowing from and flipping their criticisms. But Jammeh adopted a different style in responding to his critics. Thus, Jammeh-era and post-Jammeh political discourses are generally acerbic. Social relations under Jammeh became significantly constrained, fueled by the political strategy in which family members were used against one another for political ends. Traditional Mandinka good governance and public communication ethics frown upon aggravated speeches from leaders. Consequently, the *jalis'* roles in traditional Mandinka culture included purging aggravated or inciteful speeches before they reach the public. This is partly why traditional Mandinka leaders speak in low tones during public addresses. The strategy reinforced the *jali* as master of words.

The use of embodied cultural symbols and speech forms made Jammeh a leader who created an assortment of political accessories he could use depending on the political temperament of the country. For example, the popularity of the "*Affingjang*" musical creation by the army band became outdated by the time Jammeh solidified his image as a spiritually endowed leader. But as a relatively younger leader than Jawara, he was prone to indulge in youthful exuberance that conflicted with his "*pabe*" image. For example, as a relatively young leader, he danced in public. If Jawara was to dance in public it would feel strange to many Gambians; this was partly due to the image the public cultivated about him, which was why he was fondly called "*Baba Jawara*," "Father Jawara."

"*Alsamadi*" became a joking slogan associated with Jammeh. The pronouncement derived from how *jalis* initiate morning public or community announcements. He adopted it in zest, demonstrating his gaiety in public. People believe that Youssou Ndour's song *Alsamade* was adopted from his use of the slogan. The current music productions in the country further show how Jammeh's rule significantly impacted both the social and political rhetoric even after he left power. Witchcraft discourses in post-Jammeh Gambia took their cue from his condemned witch-hunt project, which attracted both a national and international backlash. For example, Kombonka, a youth musician, advances the witchcraft theme in his 2021 single *Buwalem*, which means "witch." People who break up families, loot public coffers, spread rumors (and those who believe those rumors), ghetto youths who snitch on the ghetto, *alkalos* who illegally sell land, officials who abuse power, those who hate truth-tellers, those who are backbiters and liars, those responsible for misgovernance, are all branded as witches in the song. The witchcraft discourse has become central to youths' political and social discourses, their concerns for justice, integrity and truth. These moral discourses appropriate or subvert different cultural motifs.

Some of the societal attitudes Jammeh's rule contributed to include the awareness of the ego in society and this is apparent in how civil discourses are constrained even among Gambia's self-identified elites, especially those in the West. Jammeh comes from the Jola ethnic group, which traditionally existed at the margins of the state. Jola people are generally thought of as loyal, hardworking and respectful. But they had limited access to education under Jawara. Like other minority ethnic groups, the types of government jobs they could access were also limited. For example, the high number of Jola recruits in The Gambia national army was a result of the structural inequalities they faced in society, and not due to any policy by Jammeh. Under Jawara, joining the army was a more accessible opportunity to people from marginalized backgrounds. This was partly because people from backgrounds with more opportunities hardly joined the army. By the time Jammeh came to power, there were already many Jolas in the lower ranks of the army. His coming to power later changed people's views about joining the army. Now, they realized it could be a means of getting to political power through a coup and this encouraged people who previously did not want to serve in the army to join it. Eventually, Jammeh appointed Jolas to senior positions in the army. But overall, the significant Jola presence in the army was a result of structural inequalities and not a result of any direct policy under Jammeh's rule.

This reality about Jolas and the army resonates with some current invented claims about Christian marginalization in Gambian public service. In contrast to what some, especially some diaspora-based Gambians argue, data on the public service shows Christians dominated Gambian public service leadership since the colonial times relative to their number. For example, the first female ambassador to be recruited in The Gambia was Ruth Sow, a Christian, who was ambassador to Belgium. Her brother, the late Ted Sow, who later converted to Islam, served as head of The Gambia Public Service Commission for many years. Sow was my personal mentor in the civil service. The first woman to be appointed as foreign minister was Susan Waffa Oggo, who served in other senior positions under the Jammeh government. The first female minister of education in The Gambia was also Christian, Louise Njie, who became the face of public education in the country during her time. Another great Christian woman, Ann Therese Ndong-Jatta, became minister of education under Jammeh. Additionally, the first female minister of finance, Margaret Keita, was a Christian, also appointed under Jammeh. In fact, focusing on gender here, Christian women have served in senior government positions that Muslim women have yet to reach. There has not been a Christian president or vice president in the country yet. However, there is no constitutional restriction that says a Christian cannot serve in those roles. It is understandable if Jammeh's proclamation about turning The Gambia into an Islamic state roused some Christian sensibilities. But this was clearly one of Jammeh's rhetoric that did not have any basis in Gambian law. Strictly and normally in Islamic law, *sharia* rules can only be applied to Muslims and not non-Muslims. This has been the case in The Gambia looking at the area of personal law, which gives both Muslims and Christians the right to conduct certain affairs based on Christian law or Islamic law, e.g. marriages and divorces, the celebration of births, dead, inheritance, etc. Overall, if one looks at the number of Christians who have served in major positions in the public sector against the number of Muslims, you will realize that the current discourse about the marginalization of Christians being pushed by certain people, especially in the diaspora, is a myth and has no basis in reality.

In The Gambia, traditionally, Muslim and Christian leaders have always worked closely together to promote inter-religious coexistence and tolerance. That practice of *"jakarlo"* and *"disso,"* to quote the late Bishop Telewa Johnson, between Muslim and Christian leaders must be maintained and revitalized in order to avoid the promotion of myths that may not serve well the interests of all Gambians or any Christian or Muslim groups.

The propagation of social and political myths have been common occurrences under the Barrow presidency. In a recent interview in July 2021, the opposition leader Ousainou Darboe disclosed that one of the biggest threats to Gambian politics was the fabrications of stories and the rampant defamation of people. His statements echo a general feeling that Gambian political culture has significantly deteriorated under President Barrow. The sentiment captures a popular Mandinka epic song on the Kaabu that laments, "fighting self-diminished the *Maaroo* people. At the height of their power, the political culture was "conquer to annihilate, bound to break up, or kill them for good." The song further mourns, "war is never easy. War confronts one with the lifeless bodies of the healthy and able-bodied, of persons of remarkable character and conduct, of friends under the untimely clutch of the cold hands of death, war is never easy."[1] The Gambia is not literally at war. But the toxicity of the current political climate can be destructive.

Hence, as the December 2021 president elections approach, there is widespread yearning for good leaders with character. Under Barrow's rule, political communication has been more "democratic" but unethical. There is the pervasive use of curse words to express political positions. This situation has stirred an appetite for appropriate leadership for the country, for the people to benefit from democracy. Jainaba Kanyi (2020), a Gambian woman, views that "Democracy is not about insults, verbal or physical fights. Democracy is like directing the citizens, on what you do for them." Democracy is shaped by good leaders. "The good leader is the one who has a good vision and goodwill for the country, ... the person has empathy and kindness for the people." Mariama Camara, another female Gambian, views that good leadership starts from the level of the family. "If a household head is aggressive, the family runs away from you, family members become agitated when they see you. If you leave the house, they are happy but when you return, they become agitated again" (Camara, 2020). For retired politician Ba Karamo Manneh, good leadership has many traits: "A good leader should have a good comportment and calmness, compassion and empathy. The indecent person or aggressive one cannot be a good leader" (Manneh, 2020). He uses Mandinka principles of leadership to further describe the attributes of a good leader: "A person should have a well-grown, mature personhood. *Hadamadinya timaringhu.* You should treat all people equally. If a leader starts dividing and ruling people, his leadership is flawed. A good leader treats equally those who like and disliked him" (Manneh, 2020). He recalled:

> When we gained independence from British colonial rule, Sir Dawda took over power when the country had very few people with proper western education. It was respect and discipline that freed this country from colonial rule. Out of unity, the elders selected leaders who in turn worked among themselves to select other leaders. This was how politics started in this country.
>
> (Manneh, 2020)

Demba Ceesay, a former Gambian educator, expressed the view that traditional social values and attitudes like tolerance and discipline, respect for authority and promoting peace among people needed to be reinforced in Gambian society (Ceesay, 2020).

Discourses about leadership and followership are channeled and shared through social media. But sometimes those discourses target specific communities or ethnicities. For example, on 29 July 2020, whatsongambia.com, a Gambian online media outlet, published a short video in which Nyang Njie, a Gambian activist charged that "everything that is bad in The Gambia is people from Banjul... Banjul people are just there to ruin the country"(Whatsongambia, 2020). Njie himself is from Banjul. He alleged Banjul people "do not have loyalty, honor, or principles. They just follow their self-interests at the expense of the national good."[2] Njie's approach to condemn an entire community is problematic in many fronts. But such discourse styles are becoming pervasive in Gambian politics. Before Njie's video surfaced, an 80-something-year-old Gambian woman in France sent a WhatsApp audio message to Marie Sock, telling her "ignore the Mandinkas, they are bas***ds." As to be expected, many Gambians – Mandinkas and non-Mandinkas – swiftly condemned the audio message (see Bojang, 2020). Sock expressed her intention to seek the presidency. The message appeared to be a *maruf* strategy communication to pit her against Mandinka people (see Introduction). Social media also enables the shaming of government officials and exposing corruption. For example, on 8 July 2020, whatongambia.com published a story about international drug smuggling in The Gambia (Saja, 2020). It alleged two Lebanese businessmen Mahdi Tajudinn and Ossama Mahmoud, smuggled 48 blocks of cocaine into the country. They were apprehended but later released by the Drug Law Enforcement Agency (DLEAG). On 1 November 2020, whatsongambia.com's Facebook page published another intriguing report.

Is The Gambia morphing into a lawless country, where people are free to do whatever they want?

Don't know whether you noticed, there is this Senegalese company that is going round throwing cables everywhere to offer TV channels at D300/monthly.

They don't have their own poles. What they do is they use NAWEC and GAMTEL poles and sometimes people's houses to attach their cables.[3]

Political debates also focus on inter-state relations. Under Barrow, many Gambians feel his regime is mortgaging the country to Senegalese business interests. The widespread insecurity in The Gambia, which has led to many cases of people being attacked in their homes, or women being gruesomely murdered or children getting missing, are making many Gambians, including former opponents of Jammeh, publicly confess that electing Barrow was a sad mistake. However, there are complex forces that have shaped Gambian politics since Barrow came to power. Notwithstanding, there is a general agreement that if the country maintains the current political climate, "*Gambia Du Dem*" ("Gambia will not go"), a metaphor for all that is wrong in Gambian political culture.

These stories from The Gambia echo the political dilemmas that Bissau-Guineans are also facing in their country. Politician João Bernardo Viera describes the current state of politics in Guinea-Bissau as follows:

> The Guinean people have a huge disappointment with the situation of the country. When people look back and see all these years we went through and we are still fighting for nothing. It means that we do not really understand the meaning of independence. We are not respecting the memories of those who fought for our independence. Many people feel let down due to the fact that Guinea-Bissau is one of the poorest countries in the world, the political actors are not getting along well, there are always fights for power.
>
> (Vieira, 2020)

For Malam Mané a, PAIGC supporter from Quinara, politics in Guinea-Bissau is no longer viable:

> Things have changed. We can support different parties now but the home front is no longer solid. There is plenty of family disputes, plenty of hatred and social strive ... serious enmity. I spent 22 years in politics. But what I thought in 2014 is very different now. Everything has resulted to disaster. There is insecurity everywhere.
>
> (Mané, 2020)

For Braima Sanhá, the degeneration of Bissau-Guinean political culture is because there is no longer "*jikko*" (meaning social confidence in Mandinka) in politics – or even in the home. In the past, we could be in different parties and remain friends. But now politics has gotten into the homes, into friendships. People have become intolerant. This is affecting social relations now (Sanhá, 2020). Another interviewee, who I call here Fafa Diallo for anonymity, thinks the problems in Guinea-Bissau are caused by a lack of morals in the state, which is also reflected by society:

> There is an erosion of honor in the state and the public service. To be honest, I do not know if it is due to the nature of politics, but people betray a lot in Guinea-Bissau. Our values are eroding. People lie to each other a lot in this country. This is a new development in society. I do not know if it is because there has been no strong democracy in the country. But in the past you dare not be in the streets and have people pointing their fingers at you saying, "this is not a serious person." People were afraid to receive social

condemnation. But now as long as they have or are making money, people do not give a damn if they receive social condemnation. All these values about honor and respect are eroding...politically, people just care about money, and being well...There is a need for a re-education of society to bring back those values of honor.

(Diallo, 2020)

Diallo believes that, as the practice of "hidden wives" become more widespread in Bissau-Guinean society, social morals are fast eroding:

Men marry officially and then they go to the side and secretly "marry" another woman or other women. These relationships are kept secret. It is now a common practice for people to have hidden wives from the public. Traditionally, you could have multiple wives but people know about them. But now they are hidden. The men codename them "my first office," "second office," "third office." This kind of relational regime is eroding social values. People trying to hide things that way is developing a lying culture which also affects social morality. If you lie at home, you will lie in society. Women have been respected in society but now this practice is also contributing to changing women. We thought our women fight for something...If you fight for anything, then you are fighting for nothing. This is affecting our society. But society is still concerned about morality.

(Diallo, 2020)

The idea that people have to fight for something alludes to the need for principles and values to guide political visions and practices. The issue of how matrimonial regimes affect politics or vice-versa is an interesting topic for future research. But a more urgent question is: why are women accepting to be "hidden concubines" when such relations are on many fronts disadvantageous to them and their children? A similar practice is also becoming common in Senegal. This means there is a need to pay urgent attention to the situation of women in society.

These yearnings and discourses explored in this chapter show citizens doubt or do not understand the purpose of the state. The extent to which citizens participate in conceiving power and establishing rules for its practices determines a lot their views of the state, its adherence to stately functions and the respectful use of power and authority. The way power and authority are performed and interrogated under the state is therefore important to the development of a leadership and a citizenry that has loyalty to the state. The good thing that is coming out of the degenerative political culture and practice is the increasing demand for moral politics. Social media is also helping to inspire the spreading of JIT movements from The Gambia, to Senegal, Guinea-Bissau to Mali and to other African contexts.

Conclusion

The trends and discontinuities in political culture and practices, the understandings of the state and the creation of political visions and aspirations are not static. This implies the state in Africa continues to evolve. There is general acceptance that widespread political and social corruption makes everyone a potential victim of such undesirable actions. Inept leadership or unethical social and economic environments or corrupted institutions all affect everyone in society. The JIT movements are mobilizing to challenge governments based on the national interest and not sectional or ethnic sentiments. These conversations about leadership and followership all depict the growing calls for a more just political culture, a more democratic political practice, and more credible institutions. They also represent a yearning for knowledge-driven political, societal and governmental systems rooted in indigenous cultures and history.

Notes

1 This song and many others have become public property and, over time, have been rendered by different *jalis* including Lalo Kebba Drammeh, the Senegambian master *Kora* player.
2 The said video was published on Whatsongambia's Facebook page and it attracted numerous comments from readers: www.facebook.com/WhatsOnGambia/, retrieved 30 July 2020. The selected comments used here have been copied verbatim. Any grammar or punctuation errors in them are reproduced as they appeared on whatsongambia's comments section below the video.
3 Whatsongambia, www.facebook.com/WhatsOnGambia, retrieved 1 November 2020.

References

Bayart, Jean-Francois, 2009. *The State in Africa: The Politics of the Belly*, Second Edition. Cambridge: Polity Press.
Bojang, Pa Modou. 2020. "Pa Modou Bojang on Marie Sock." Mengbekering Radio on Youtube.

Cabral, Amilcar. 1979. *Unity and Struggle. Speeches and Writings of Amilcar Cabral. Monthly Review Press Classics.* Guinea-Bissau: PAIGC.

Camara, Mariama. 2020. Interview with author, 26 July.

Ceesay, Demba. 2020. Interview with author, 3 December.

Diallo, Fafa. 2020. Interview with author, 19 July.

Englebert, Pierre. 2020. Interview with author, 17 August

Gambia Daily. 1996a. "Commit yourself to God, says Bishop Michael Cleary." *Gambia Daily Newspaper*, 3 January, No. 150, p. 2.

Gambia Daily. 1996b. "Voices from the Past, 30 years ago from the Gambia New Bulletin, 1st March 1966." *Gambia Daily Newspaper*, 1 March, No. 173, p. 8.

Government of The Gambia. 1980. *The Gambia Since Independence:1965– 1980, Fifteen Years of Nationhood*, 1–15.

Kanyi, Jainaba. 2020. Interview with author, 26 July.

Karibe Mendy, Peter. 2020. Interview with author, 10 August.

Khan, Mariama. 2016. "Indigenous Languages and Africa's Development Dilemma." In *Endogenous Development, Naïve romanticism or practical route to sustainable African development*, edited by Chiku Malunga and Susan H. Holcombe, pp. 150–162. London: Routledge.

Khan, Mariama. 2019. *The Gambia–Senegal Border, Issues in Regional Integration, Routledge Borderland Studies*. London & New York: Routledge.

Khan, Mariama (unpublished). "How threats to entitlements, ethnicity, minority nationalism, Casamance rebellion and Structural Adjustment collapsed the Senegambia Confederation, 1982–1989.

Mané, Malam. 2020. Interview with author, 19 July.

Manjang, Ousmane. 1983: "Ten Years Since the Muder of Matarr Sarr." *Bantaba in Cyberspace Gambia.* October.

Manneh, Ba Karamo. 2020. Interview with author, 26 July.

Mkandawire, T. and C. C. Soludo. 1999. *Our Continent, Our Future: African Perspectives on Structural Adjustment.* New Jersey, Asmara: Africa World Press.

Saja. 2020. "Cocaine in The Gambia: Are Lebanese Traffickers Above the law." http://whatson-gambia.com/index.php/news/2944-cocaine-in-the-gambia-are-lebanese-traffickers-above-the-law?tmpl=component&componentStyle=blog_3&print=1&layout=default, 8 July. Retrieved 31 July.

Sanhá, Braima. 2021. Interview with author, 19 July.

Sanyang, Sulayman. 2020. Interviews with author, 5 July–8 August.

Somerville, Carolyn M. 1991. The Impact of Reforms on the Urban Population: How the Dakarois view the Crisis. In *The Political Economy of Senegal under Structural Adjustment*, edited by C. L. Delgado and S. Jammeh, p. 152. New York: Praeger Publishers.

Touray, Suntu. 2014. "Ousman Manjang, A Tragic Story That Rocks Banjul Ten years since the murder of Matarr Sarr, The late Saul Samba shot by his best Friend Matarr Sarr," Stockholm, October 1983, *Kaironews.com*.

Vieira, João Bernardo. 2020. Interview with author, 17 and 19 July.

Whatsongambia. 2020. "Nyang Njie attacks Banjulians!" www.facebook.com/ WhatsOnGambia/. Rretrieved 30 July 2020.

Index

124   *Index*

colonial leaders of 3; as colonial
state 84–89; current state of
politics in 118–120; diaspora
from 8–9; economic policy
in 108–109; independence of
3–4; Justice, Integrity and Truth
(JIT) movement in 1–2, 4–5,
8–9; Mandinkas founding of 2–3;
moral issues in 118–119; music of
29–30; naked body politics in 22;
nation building after colonialism
89–94; political disenchantment in
1–2; political parties in 85–89, 94;
respect for elders in 87

Haar, G. t. 18, 24–25, 44, 46
Harris, N. 27
Herbst, J. I. 94
hidden wives 119
Hitler, A. 79
Holcombe, S. H. 72
Huxley, E. 75

indigenous theory 26
International Monetary Fund (IMF)
103
Islamic state, Gambia as 111,
115

jalis 47–50
Jammeh, M. T. 14; Christians serving
under 114–115; cultural symbols
and speech forms used by 113
Jammeh, Y. 5–8, 75, 108; claim to
be descendant of Mama Tamba
Jammeh 14; political rhetoric
under 109–113
Jan, B. 63
Janneh, F. W. 84
Jawara, D. K. 80–82, 92–93, 97; break
from colonial vision for Gambia
101–102; commercial relations
under 103; personal *jali* of 98, 105;
rebellion against 104–105; in songs
106–107
Jobarteh, A. B. 98
Johnson, T. 115
Justice, Integrity and Truth (JIT)
movements 1–2, 4–5, 8–9, 100;

democracy and 27; redefining
African politics 37

Kaabu 2, 17; arranged marriages
among 57–58; collapse of 72;
founding of 41–43; government
and state institutions in 50–52;
influence on Gambia and Guinea-
Bissau 37–38, 97–98; leadership
protocols among 44; and
Mandinka origins 39–41; Muslims
of 52; political legitimacy of
17–25; shrines of 45–46; spiritual
endowments of leaders of 44–45;
statecraft among 43–50; values of
47; women and youth in 52–60
Kabunka people 58–59
Kanteh, S. 41
Kanyi, J. 116
Keita, I. B. 4
Keita, M. 114–115
Keita, S. 18
Kendall, M. 74
Khan, F. 103
Konateh, M. 62
Kula, M. B. 52
Kuyateh, F. 98
Kuyateh, J. 29, 52–53

Labe, A. M. 68
Laye, S. L. 16
legitimacy, political: Kabunka 17–25;
morality and 11–17
Lennox-Boyd, A. 83
liberal democracy 26–27
Liberia 16
Lumumba, P. 21

Maal, B. 29
Madi, S. 102–103
Mahmoud, O. 117
Mahoney, J. 80
Mali 1, 2, 4, 36, 40; demand for moral
leadership in 33; demonstrations
against leaders of 4; history of
38, 39–40; Justice, Integrity and
Truth (JIT) movement in 18; socio-
religious groups in 25; state-society
relations in 27
Mamdani, M. 28

For Product Safety Concerns and Information please contact our EU
representative GPSR@taylorandfrancis.com
Taylor & Francis Verlag GmbH, Kaufingerstraße 24, 80331 München, Germany

www.ingramcontent.com/pod-product-compliance
Lightning Source LLC
Chambersburg PA
CBHW061750270326
41928CB00011B/2444

9 780367 690069